DARE

TO FOLLOW

Charlotte Gambill & Natalie Grant

HARVEST HOUSE PUBLISHERS
EUGENE. OREGON

Cover design by Faceout Studio, Jeff Miller

Interior design by KUHN Design Group

For bulk, special sales, or ministry purchases, please call 1-800-547-8979.
Email: Customerservice@hhpbooks.com

Dare to Follow
Copyright © 2022 by Charlotte Gambill and Natalie Grant
Published by Harvest House Publishers
Eugene, Oregon 97408
www.harvesthousepublishers.com

ISBN 978-0-7369-8458-4 (pbk)
ISBN 978-0-7369-8459-1 (eBook)

Library of Congress Control Number: 2021949285

Printed in the United States of America

22 23 24 25 26 27 28 29 30 / VP / 10 9 8 7 6 5 4 3 2 1

CONTENTS

TWO WORDS TO CHANGE YOUR LIFE

---

*As Jesus walked beside the Sea of Galilee, he saw Simon
and his brother Andrew casting a net into the lake, for
they were fishermen. "Come, follow me," Jesus said.*

MARK 1:16-17

ollow me. Those two words were about to change everything for the ones who were brave enough to respond. Jesus didn't give instructions, just two words of invitation. They were the only words He spoke as He dared them to take the next step. He didn't answer any questions the disciples may have had about where they were going or why they should follow Him. He did not hand out a job brief and a benefits package to entice them to leave all they had ever known to follow a man they had just met. *Follow me* was the entryway to the greatest adventure they could ever dare to discover, but it was also the starting place of a lifetime of surrender. *Follow me* was not simply pointing to a destination; it was all about a decision. The disciples' future was unknown, but their direction was certain.

In a world that seems obsessed with following, we can find ourselves confused and challenged by which direction to go. The people and trends who shout, "Follow me!" can drown out the significance of that decision. Our following is not incidental, it is fundamental. The voices we follow shape the choices we make. Who or what we follow shapes the life we are building. That's why following isn't just a one-time decision; it's a daily commitment. The disciples responded to the initial invitation, but like us, they then had to continue daily to act on that decision.

We can so easily forget that we are called to follow first. We are so busy with life we often take the lead and later—usually when things are not working out, or when the pressure mounts—we want to switch back the control from our way to following His ways. This devotional was written to encourage you to get back to the place where you can say *yes* again to the invitation to follow Jesus. Dare to follow His ways and dare to unfollow what has begun to confuse and block the way. Dare to surrender and say, as the old song so beautifully puts it: *I have decided to follow Jesus, no turning back, no turning back.*

*The voices we follow
shape the choices we make.*

HOW TO USE THIS DEVOTIONAL

We get it! Life can get busy, and committing to doing a daily devotional can feel overwhelming. If you miss a day, you feel bad and maybe even think about giving up. Well, friend, we are here cheering you on. We have written this devotional in a way that we know works for us in our lives, and we hope it works for you too.

This is a 100-day journey, one we pray you will find has a pace and ease to it that helps your following find a flow. We are going to dare you to follow and then give you the space to process and journal your response.

In James 1:22, we are told: "Do not merely listen to the word, and so deceive yourselves. Do what it says." We want to encourage you to hear but also to then do something that will help you follow through. We have split the book up into five sections, each with 20 devotionals. On one day you'll read a few lines of challenge and encouragement from us, and on the next day you'll be invited to respond to that invitation through journaling and prayer. On your day of study, we pray that God will speak to your heart. On the day of follow-through, we pray that you will begin to take steps that will bring these words to life.

So, friend, as you are about to begin, let's pray together:

Thank You, Jesus, for leading me to this moment.
Thank You that You have made a way for me in every season.
Lord, help me as I commit to this study
to surrender what is in the way so that
You can truly have Your way.
Lord, make alive Your Word in my life.
Lord, help me not just to be a hearer of the Word but also a doer.
Lord, I commit afresh today to follow You all the days of my life.
Amen.

PART ONE

DARE
TO
FOLLOW

WHO'S FOLLOWING WHOM?

—— *Charlotte* ——

When he was twelve years old, they went up to the festival, according to the custom. After the festival was over, while his parents were returning home, the boy Jesus stayed behind in Jerusalem, but they were unaware of it.

LUKE 2:42-43

Can you imagine losing Jesus? I've lost my car keys and a wallet, and that caused enough panic. But imagine that you suddenly realized you had lost the Savior of the world. That's what happened to Mary and Joseph.

They had been to the Passover with all their family, as they did every year. Only on this occasion, something shifted. When it came time to head home, Jesus knew it was His time to stop following everyone else's lead. It was His turn to follow that course His Father had predestined for Him. Jesus knew He didn't need to follow Mary and Joseph to their house; He needed to be the one who was found in the Father's house. Mary and Joseph assumed Jesus was following them, but in fact, the time had come for them to start following Him.

We can get so used to being in control, to being the one to plan the trip or get the group together. Our ability to get it done can mean we actually prefer to dominate so we get the outcome we want. However, for real growth to happen, we have to discern when it is time to follow. The timing caught Mary and Joseph off guard: They assumed that Jesus would be following them; they didn't even consider that they could lose Him.

In our spiritual journey, we have to constantly stop and assess: Who is following whom? We can set off closely following Jesus, aware of our need for His direction and guidance, stopping regularly to hear His voice and lean into His wisdom. Yet as confidence and familiarity increase, we can just as easily replace our following with being the one who expects others to follow us. Our voice becomes louder than His; we expect God to bless the direction we are heading; we are presumptuous where before we were cautious. Without even being aware of the change, we can follow our own ideas instead of the One who said, "Follow me."

As we prepare to spend the next 100 days reflecting on what it means to follow Christ, let's begin with the most important question. Today, who is following whom? Is it time to surrender control and become a follower again? Who's taking the lead in your emotional, relational, and spiritual life? Is He in front, or, without even realizing it, have we left His words, wisdom, and ways behind?

Everything changes when we follow Jesus. Our priorities, our perspective, and our passions. Our willingness to surrender control is the beginning of our commitment to follow.

Who's taking the lead in your emotional, relational, and spiritual life? Prayerfully discern which voices you've been following and ask God to show you how worldly wisdom differs from His Word.

THE COST OF FOLLOWING

—— *Charlotte* ——

Suppose a king is about to go to war against another king. Won't he first sit down and consider whether he is able with ten thousand men to oppose the one coming against him with twenty thousand?

LUKE 14:31

When I was a student and moved away from home, I suddenly had to budget for my food and bills each week. I remember going to the grocery store to get some of the things my mum stocked our cupboards with back home. As the cashier scanned my items, I realized I didn't have enough money for everything in my shopping cart. This embarrassing moment taught me that before I went to pay for the items, I needed to make sure I could afford them. I also learned that just because the items were in my mum's cupboard, that didn't mean I automatically got them in mine.

In a world where we can envy what others have, a realization of the cost they have paid to help us grow should give us a deeper appreciation and respect for one another. When I would return home on summer break from university,

I would have a newfound gratitude for the things I had previously taken for granted. I would open the fridge and it would be full of my favorite food—but now I didn't just see food. I saw someone's hard work and commitment to provide.

Everything has a cost. The disciples, at the invitation to follow Jesus, immediately experienced this cost as they left their boats, left their businesses, left their communities and families. Before anything else happened, before any of the miracles or sermons, the disciples felt the cost of following. What they didn't understand in that moment was how it paled in comparison to the cost Jesus would pay to follow His Father's will to the cross.

Following Jesus will cost us in this life. But praise be to Jesus that He has paid the ultimate and complete price! You can count the cost gladly because it's true that He satisfies every desire you could want to add to your life. Seeing Jesus increase in your life brings about a fullness of joy that is worth every change you could embrace. You can dare to count the cost of following the One who paid it all for you.

_____

Have you ever experienced

a cost to following Jesus?

What was your

response to this cost?

THE PROXIMITY OF FOLLOWING

———— *Natalie* ————

*Father, I want those you have given me to be with me
where I am, and to see my glory, the glory you have given me
because you loved me before the creation of the world.*

JOHN 17:24

The best thing about social media is how it allows us to stay closer and more connected with friends who don't live in close physical proximity to us. We have the ability to follow along as they get married, raise their children, experience loss, receive a promotion at work, or achieve a life goal of theirs. This is just one way we can maintain a close proximity to one another. What's true online and offline is that unless you show up and work to maintain a relationship, the connection will flounder.

In John 15, Jesus emphasizes the importance of our proximity to Him in our journey of following Him. "I am the vine; you are the branches. If you remain in me and I in you, you will bear much fruit; apart from me you can do nothing" (verse 5). We're not just talking about staying connected on social media, an occasional catching up over coffee, or even the closeness you might experience with a spouse. It's an everyday, consistent choice to be in the closest proximity to Him—remaining *in* Him and He *in* you. You can't get any closer than that! But if we choose not to remain and be intentional about our connection, we experience more than FOMO (the fear of missing out) in social settings. The Word says we're literally unable to bear good fruit or do anything unless we are connected to Him.

We can't move forward or follow Jesus if we aren't remaining in Him. And what does it look like to remain? Think about how many different ways there are to stay connected to those we are close to! We can talk on the phone, send text messages, go on trips, comment on social media, send a note in the mail, or sit in the same room. It always takes more than one type of connection to really make it work, and the same is true when it comes to staying connected to the Vine. Our relationship with Jesus includes times of prayer, getting into His Word, worshipping in song, and sitting in His presence.

In one of His last prayers before He goes to the cross, we read how Jesus prays to the Father saying, "I want those you have given me to be with me where I am" (John 17:24). As we continue in our journey of following Jesus, we can be sure that it's not just us wanting to be close to Him; He wants to be close to us too. As we reach for Him, He is reaching for us.

DAY 6

What activities or practices help you feel most connected to God? If you've been feeling disconnected, what does God promise about His presence and nearness in your life?

THE CHALLENGE OF FOLLOWING

—— *Charlotte* ——

*Father, if you are willing, take this cup from
me; yet not my will, but yours be done.*

LUKE 22:42

ot my will but Yours. We'd like to say the same of our lives—that we follow God's will, not our own—but most days, this verse is a challenge. Many times, we find ourselves at the intersection of His will or our will. The deciding vote determines what we follow next, and we can be overwhelmed with options and opinions. So how do you ensure you're following His will and not your own?

We can overcomplicate the will of God. God isn't setting us an impossible challenge; instead, He is giving us a calling and directive within which we make choices. God's will is for us to follow Him and for our lives to be a reflection of Him. He wants us to carry the good news of His kingdom and to be a conduit of kindness and blessing to the world around us. Those small daily decisions all stem from our agreement with God about the direction of our lives.

In Deuteronomy 30:19-20, God tells the people of Israel,

> "I have set before you life and death, blessings and curses. Now choose life, so that you and your children may live and that you may love the LORD your God, listen to his voice, and hold fast to him. For the LORD is your life."

We have the power to choose, and choosing God's way, following God's Word, brings our everyday life into agreement with His will.

We face a constant tug in our hearts and minds to turn from God's will. But God is gracious towards us. He wants us to learn and mature, to grow in our confidence of knowing how to live in His will.

Today, if you feel challenged as you follow Jesus, take a step back. Instead of making it about the small things, look at the bigger picture. When you are hurt or have been betrayed, your will says: *be offended, retaliate*. But God's will says: *forgive, release*. What lines up with the heart of God? What most reflects His nature and goodness? The challenge to following may be resolved as you pray this prayer: *Not my will but Yours be done.*

Reflect on a choice or decision

you're confronting this week.

What would be the outcome

of following the world's

wisdom? What would happen

if you chose God's way?

DAY 9

FOLLOWING VERSUS FEELINGS

—— Natalie ——

Simon Peter answered him, "Lord, to whom shall we go?
You have the words of eternal life."

JOHN 6:68

I f something feels confusing or we're not sure how it might work out for us, we tend to back away rather than remain consistent or lean in closer. We like to take our time, do our research, know exactly what we're committing to before we go all in.

In John 6, we see how some of the disciples who had been following Jesus found one of His teachings difficult to understand and accept. Because of this, many of His disciples turned away and stopped following Him. Rather than leaning in, fixing their eyes on Jesus, and persevering through something difficult to experience something glorious, they chose to follow their feelings away from Jesus.

After this, Jesus turned to the 12 disciples and asked if they wanted to leave too. That's when Peter responded by saying, "Lord, to whom shall we go?"

What's important is how Peter doesn't comment on Jesus' teaching, his level of understanding, or how confusing it feels; instead, he declares what is true. Jesus has the words of eternal life, and that life extends far beyond what Peter sees, feels, or understands in the moment. So Peter just says, "We have come to believe and to know that you are the Holy One of God" (verse 69).

In this life, we're often faced with confusing situations or hard teachings, and it's up to us to decide if we will commit ourselves to God's truth or follow our feelings to avoid what seems difficult. In the midst of our confusion, we can rest in the truth that Jesus offers eternal life and a freedom that extends far beyond what we see, feel, or understand right in front of us. Ephesians 3:20 says that God is able to do "immeasurably more than all we ask or imagine." Our inability to understand what God might be doing is an indicator that it's *more* than what we can comprehend.

Perhaps you've been following your feelings and you know it's not the best road to travel, or maybe you're tempted to give in to what feels good right now. Let me encourage you with this promise from God's Word: "Let us not become weary in doing good, for at the proper time we will reap a harvest if we do not give up" (Galatians 6:9). When you continue to fix your eyes on Jesus, even when it doesn't feel good, you *will* reap a harvest!

Have you ever experienced

a time when you reaped

a harvest because of your

commitment to God's truth?

How have you already

seen the results of your

submission to His will?

FOLLOWING WHEN YOU'RE BUSY

—— *Natalie* ——

Since we are surrounded by such a great cloud of witnesses, let us throw off everything that hinders and the sin that so easily entangles. And let us run with perseverance the race marked out for us, fixing our eyes on Jesus, the pioneer and perfecter of faith.

HEBREWS 12:1-2

Have you ever traveled with your family during a busy travel day at the airport? The goal is to follow one another through the crowd, get to your gate, and ultimately to your travel destination. There's always a lot going on at the airport, though. It's easy to get distracted and lose focus. Every airport is different when it comes to taking your shoes off or keeping them on when you walk through security, announcements are being made on the loudspeaker, and the crowds of people move around at their own pace. That's not to mention the shops, music, and smell of fast food filling the atmosphere. If you don't stay focused on who you're with and where you're going, you might look up and find the person you had mindlessly been following as you looked longingly over your shoulder at the Chick-fil-A breakfast menu is not, in fact, part of your group.

Following Jesus can feel the same way when things pick up at work or your kids' social calendars introduce you to a new role as a chauffeur. When life gets busier, we tend to put long-term priorities aside, focusing on the small tasks to make sure we aren't forgetting anything. The danger is, we might look up a few months later and realize we're not where we should be. We fixed our eyes on the short term and found ourselves dangerously off-course.

Hebrews 12 is a powerful reminder for us to keep our eyes fixed on Jesus. Having a full schedule isn't a bad thing. Working harder and going after a job promotion or adding another activity to the social calendar are all just part of life, and they're often steps along the way in fulfilling the call God has on our lives. But they become a hindrance when we take our eyes off Jesus and focus on the new job title or social status. We must learn to view all our busyness in light of who He is, the pioneer and perfecter of our faith. His Word promises that if we keep our eyes fixed on Him, we will never be led astray.

Reflect on a time when you allowed short-term priorities to obscure a long-term goal. How did God redirect you?

FOLLOWING WHEN NOTHING IS MOVING

—— Charlotte ——

*Remain in me, as I also remain in you. No branch can
bear fruit by itself; it must remain in the vine. Neither
can you bear fruit unless you remain in me.*

JOHN 15:4

ave you ever been driving down the freeway and run into a huge traffic jam? You can't move anywhere, and your GPS has fallen silent. You're stuck in traffic, but no other routes are showing up. All you can see are the taillights ahead of you.

Following where God is leading can feel just like that traffic jam. We were making good progress, found a flow, and were following what we felt called to do. Then suddenly we hit a roadblock, and everything comes to a halt. It's in these moments spiritually when we can begin to struggle, because we have associated following God with forward movement. Yet oftentimes, following is more about remaining and being still than it is about climbing and conquering.

When the heavens are silent and the direction is unclear, we can trust that the last instruction God gave us is the same instruction that will still help us. We read in John 6 of when the disciples were told to set off for Capernaum but Jesus didn't go with them. As they sailed across the Sea of Galilee, a storm hit. Jesus had to join them, walking on the water, to remind them that the place He had directed them was still the destination. They were to follow the same instruction even though the circumstances looked different.

Remaining on our course requires us to trust the silence as much as we trust the shout. When you are in that traffic jam, your GPS may stop talking as it knows you are not currently moving, but it's still logged in to where you are going. Dare to trust the GPS of the Holy Spirit. Dare to remain at your post, to remain steadfast, to trust that still small voice. Dare to know that the movement and the pace of your life is not the measure of your commitment to Christ. At times, following God when nothing is happening is the boldest thing you can do.

How many times have we given up because of a temporary setback or holdup? Remaining in Him means you won't let the traffic jam change your life plans. So today, if it feels like nothing is moving, commit to staying on course, knowing God is moving in the stillness.

Describe a season of waiting in your life. How did God remain faithful even when it felt like your momentum was stalled?

FOLLOWING WITH A GOOD ATTITUDE

Natalie

Each of you should give what you have decided in your heart to give,
not reluctantly or under compulsion, for God loves a cheerful giver.

2 CORINTHIANS 9:7

It's never fun to receive a gift someone feels obligated to give you, even if it's something you really want or need. The lack of enthusiasm deflates the excitement of the gift. Whether it's an apology or a helping hand, if we sense that it's not freely given, we almost don't even want it. Why show up for it if you're going to be miserable about it? I've experienced this many times in work settings, sometimes in other people and sometimes even within myself, where we show up to the job we've agreed to *and get paid for*, but we walk around complaining about the work we've been asked to do. Even though we may be accomplishing the tasks set before us, a poor attitude shifts the atmosphere.

Maybe God has you in a job you don't enjoy. Perhaps loving and submitting to your husband feels like you're making a bigger sacrifice than he is. Or maybe you've been obedient for a long time and you're just not seeing any shift in your circumstances. Sometimes what God calls us to is hard or boring or doesn't feel fair to us. In these times, I think about Jonah. When he finally obeys God, he goes to the city of Nineveh and delivers the message he's received from the Lord. The whole city repents and worships God. You'd think Jonah would be a little more cheerful about being part of how much glory God received through him, but the story ends with Jonah feeling angry. He showed up for what God called him to do, but the whole experience was bitter for him because he showed up with a poor attitude.

Even if we don't understand what God is doing or why He's asking us to do it, we can still move along in our journey with excitement and expectation. When Scripture tells us that we should cheerfully give what we've decided in our hearts to give, it doesn't just apply to financial giving. This message applies to everything we've decided in our hearts to give. If we give our lives to Christ and choose to follow Him, then we should do so cheerfully and not reluctantly.

The good news is that we're not doing this on our own. We don't have to muster up our own excitement or enthusiasm. Following Jesus isn't just about being obedient and simply accomplishing a task. It's about remaining in Him, in His presence, throughout the process. When you spend time in His presence, that's when you're able to bear the fruit of the Spirit. His presence is what equips you to be able to show up with love, joy, peace, patience, kindness, goodness, faithfulness, gentleness, and self-control.

Reflect on two situations—a time when you showed up with a positive attitude, and a time when you struggled to muster any enthusiasm for the task before you. How were the outcomes of your circumstances different? How did your attitude reflect God's Spirit within you?

FOLLOWING INTO THE FIRE

—— *Natalie* ——

*The LORD answered, "I will be with you, and you will strike
down all the Midianites, leaving none alive."*

JUDGES 6:16

When we think about following Jesus, we love to imagine amazing, miraculous experiences. My mind always goes straight to the "mountaintop moments"—a new record deal, or a speaking opportunity that will allow me to be part of what God is doing in the lives of others in a powerful way. The Bible is full of promises of those victories, but we don't often consider what the journey to those moments looks like. More often than not, the path looks strange and confusing and even a little unsafe or unwise to us. Have you ever had a moment where God led you into a situation you had no idea how you would get out of? It can feel pretty scary and intimidating to continue boldly moving forward with Him! Thankfully, we're not alone, and we have plenty of testimonies to draw courage from. We know God keeps His promises!

In Judges 6, God picks Gideon to be the one to deliver the Israelites from the hand of Midian. After receiving confirmation that it was, in fact, God speaking to him, Gideon is ready to move forward and receive that victory! But as he and his men are ready to go, God tells Gideon he has too many men, even though they were already outnumbered. Ultimately, Gideon's army is reduced to a mere 300 men. It doesn't take a soldier to understand there is strength in numbers, and downsizing an army sounds more like asking for defeat than arming for victory. But how much more glory does God receive when we watch Him do the miraculous? Sometimes we're stripped of our own strength, but it's not because God has abandoned us. It's because He wants to do something even greater, showing His strength through our weakness.

We rarely get to know the plan beyond what we see in front of us, but God gives us this promise: He will be with us. When things are looking up and we're experiencing miraculous provision, or when our situation becomes dire and we're not sure we'll make it through, we always have the presence of God and the power that comes with it.

When Shadrach, Meshach, and Abednego were thrown into a literal fire for refusing to bow down and worship King Nebuchadnezzar's golden statue in Daniel 3, God was with them and they were untouched by the flames. Scripture describes how "the fire had not harmed their bodies, nor was a hair of their heads singed; their robes were not scorched, and there was no smell of fire on them." Our worship and obedience may bring us into situations that make us think, *This can't be right.* But no matter how tight of a spot we find ourselves in, we can trust that God will be with us, and "what is impossible with man is possible with God" (Luke 18:27).

Describe a time you tried to

operate in your own strength.

How did God lead you to

depend on Him, showing His

power through your weakness?

FOLLOWING IN THE DARK

—— *Charlotte* ——

Your word is a lamp for my feet, a light on my path.

PSALM 119:105

It's probably an age thing but over the last few years, I've found driving at night far more difficult than driving in the day. The headlights in my eyes, navigating unfamiliar places in the fading light…it all adds extra pressure. What I could see clearly in the daylight is hard to discern in the dark. There are times on our life journey when following Jesus feels just like this. But when circumstances are dark, God's Word will illuminate the path before us.

The days following the crucifixion of Jesus were dark days for His disciples. They believed that darkness had won and hope was lost. They felt disoriented, unsure how to follow when the One whom they had been following was no longer present. They drifted; some left town, heading back on the road to Emmaus. And on that road, Jesus showed up. As they talked about the darkness of their situation, Jesus entered the narrative and turned on the light. He began reminding them of the Word of God. Although they didn't recognize Jesus, they sensed the light of a fire in the midst of their doubt and fear:

> They asked each other, "Were not our hearts burning within us while he talked with us on the road and opened the Scriptures to us?" (Luke 24:32).

His Word brings light in the darkest of moments. In times of hopelessness, it takes your mind from the path of disappointment and onto the path of what's possible with God. In times of anxiety, it replaces panic with peace. Your perspective is lifted higher to the Heavenly Father who cares for you and who carries your burdens (Matthew 11:28-29).

Dark seasons can affect our vision and they can confuse our sense of direction. So when it's dark, we need to adjust our speed. We need to slow down the pace so we can ensure we don't lose our way. We can't depend on our own vision, so we need to slow down to discern the voice of the Holy Spirit within us, burning with conviction and clarity, guiding us along the right path.

If it's dark in your world right now, turn up the light. Turn up the truth of God's Word; put on the floodlights of His promises and truth. Don't allow the shadows to overwhelm or intimidate you. When it's dark, shine the truth and you will once again find the path to follow.

Does any situation in your life seem dark and overwhelming? How does God's Word illuminate the path forward? Choose a verse of Scripture that reminds you of God's guidance and promises and commit it to memory today.

PART TWO

SIGNS OF A LIFE THAT'S FOLLOWING

FOLLOWING LOVE

—— Charlotte ——

We know and rely on the love God has for us. God is love.
Whoever lives in love lives in God, and God in them.

1 JOHN 4:16

In a world that constantly wants to define what love looks like and sounds like, understanding the concept of love can be confusing. Love is portrayed as an overwhelming emotional bond, as a sentimental gesture, as a romantic destination or inevitable heartbreak. We are shown what love should look like and told what it should feel like. Yet following love that is defined by anything other than the One who is love will only ever leave us disappointed.

Life can only find true meaning when we follow the ways of love Jesus modeled for us in Scripture. Loving like Jesus loved isn't a gimmick or an emotion; it's a decision that requires devotion. Perhaps that's why we so often settle for the world's version of love rather than the true love we find in the Living Word.

Are you loving the way Jesus loved? Today, commit to addressing just one of the aspects of what this kind of love looks like and sounds like. The list may feel long, but the benefits of following this love are eternal:

Love is patient, love is kind. It does not envy, it does not boast, it is not proud. It does not dishonor others, it is not self-seeking, it is not easily angered, it keeps no record of wrongs. Love does not delight in evil but rejoices with the truth. It always protects, always trusts, always hopes, always perseveres. Love never fails (1 Corinthians 13:4-8).

Have you lost one of those attributes of love? Where do you need to start following again? Has your love lost patience; has it begun to be unkind? Has your love become self-centered or jealous? Remember, love rarely has anything to do with your momentary feelings. It has to do with your faithfulness. This love is for all weather, and it protects in every season. God loved you like this when He gave His only Son for you. If you follow the love that saved you, you will begin to model a love that will sacrifice for others.

The discovery of real love will leave you determined not to settle for a poor substitute. Let your life follow love; visit the depths and explore the heights. The love of God never fails, and it's so vast you cannot measure it. That's the kind of love you are called to pursue.

Read 1 Corinthians 13:4-8.

This is a familiar passage, so

read it slowly, taking the time to

digest the meaning of the words.

How have you experienced

this kind of love in your life?

In what ways can you choose

to reflect it to others today?

DAY 23

FOLLOWING TRUTH

—— *Natalie* ——

Jesus answered, "I am the way and the truth and the life.
No one comes to the Father except through me."

JOHN 14:6

If you look up the definition of the word *truth* in the dictionary, you will
find that a belief or an idea that is *accepted* as true is included as truth.
This is where we get "my truth" and "your truth," and it's where the line
between fact and perception becomes blurred. At this point, we're splitting hairs
about word definition, but it's important to remember that the truth Jesus is
referring to in today's verse isn't merely "widely accepted as true," or something
that makes sense based on what you can see. We're not talking about subjective
ideas that depend on circumstance or situation, but the ultimate, unchanging
truth that exists above all else: the truth of Jesus.

In John 14, when Jesus' disciples ask Him how they could know "the way"
to the place He was going, Jesus responds with a statement: He is the way, the
truth, and the life. He covers all the bases as He explains that the way to the
Father is through Him. He is not just the pathway, but in Him is where truth
and life are found. All three work together.

Following truth means to follow the way of Jesus and experience life in Him. There is a higher reality and a greater power and authority than what we can see in front of us. Philippians 2:9 tells us that God elevated Jesus to the highest place and gave Him the name that is above every name. No matter what you're facing or what it's named, the name of Jesus is above it all.

When we're faced with difficult situations in life and the circumstances don't look promising, we have a choice to make. We can stay stuck in a limited definition of truth that is dictated by what we can see right in front of us. Or we can deeply follow Truth and declare the name of Jesus over our situation, calling the details of our circumstance into alignment with what He promises in His Word. It's not a denial or an avoidance of reality, and we should respond to our physical needs with wisdom, but we don't need to bow lower to meet the facts. We are keeping our head up and pointing to Jesus, the ultimate authority—the Way, the Truth, and the Life.

_____

Is there a circumstance in your life that you've struggled to bring into alignment with God's Word? What might it look like for you to give Jesus authority over that situation? How could the reality of His truth change your perceptions?

FOLLOWING PEACE

—— *Charlotte* ——

The peace of God, which transcends all understanding,
will guard your hearts and your minds in Christ Jesus.

PHILIPPIANS 4:7

Sit for a moment and imagine *peace.* What do you envision? Perhaps it's escaping to a spa or a retreat center. That sounds like a great idea, but it's an expensive commitment every time your world gets noisy. The truth is, the peace we are called to pursue is not external, it's internal. The peace we are called to follow is not fragile, it's fortified.

I want to tell you something very important that you mustn't forget: The enemy cannot manufacture peace. It's impossible: He cannot give you peace because he has no peace to give. Do you know why? Because our Jesus is the Prince of Peace. So even in the most testing times, if we follow the leading of the Prince of Peace, He will allow us to sleep in the storm.

Have you ever been in a really difficult situation and as you have prayed, you have been overwhelmed by a sense of peace? Even though your outward circumstances weren't changing—maybe they even became more challenging—you had peace. That's the peace God wants us to follow. When we follow that peace, we make the right decisions to advance even though everything around us says *retreat*. When we trust that peace, we don't jump ship because we know the storm will pass.

The peace that Daniel had in God being his source, his provider and protector, meant he could be thrown into a lions' den without a sign of panic. We read in Daniel 6 that he went in peace into the place where a roaring predator could have torn him apart, and the predator became his pillow. How do we find that peace? Well, like Daniel, we have to stop listening to the wrong voices. We have to shut out the opinions that come from those who have no peace. Instead, we need to give ourselves over to God's peace.

So often the panic gets more room than the peace. In Matthew 8, we read that Jesus slept in the storm. The peace that was within Him was very different from the noise that surrounded Him. To follow peace, we need to surrender our will; the fight over who gets the real estate in your mind determines how much room peace has to reside.

Who do you follow in the storm? Who is the one you grab ahold of when things feel like they are out of control? When you feel God-given peace, follow it; the enemy has no way to make a counterfeit. Let His peace lead you beyond where the lies want to keep you.

What does peace mean to you? Describe a situation in which you felt calm, certainty, and trust in God's provision, even in the midst of difficult circumstances. What brought you those feelings of peace?

FOLLOW WISDOM

—— *Charlotte* ——

The beginning of wisdom is this: Get wisdom.
Though it cost all you have, get understanding.

PROVERBS 4:7

Proverbs 9 paints a picture of Wisdom as a woman who stands and calls to us to come and sit at her table. On the same street corner, another woman, Folly, is also looking for dinner guests. These two voices have very different agendas and lead to very different places. So why is it that we so often struggle to choose Wisdom over Folly?

We can get very used to the ways of Folly; she can become a familiar friend that we feel reluctant to be parted from. The table of Wisdom calls for a different mindset. Wisdom will ask you to change your spiritual diet, and she will challenge your table manners, but ultimately, Wisdom is the friend we should follow.

The Bible tells us exactly how we can increase our wisdom:

If any of you lacks wisdom, you should ask God, who gives generously to all without finding fault, and it will be given to you (James 1:5).

Often, we would rather try to figure something out on our own than ask for help. But God wants us to ask for wisdom for every part of our lives: our family, our finances, our friendships. We have to be willing to follow where Wisdom leads. Wisdom is a constant companion. She is not someone you visit occasionally; she has to become the company you keep. So how often are you walking with Wisdom? Do you have people in your life with whom you walk because you want to learn from the wisdom they carry?

Proverbs 9:10 tells us that the fear of the Lord is the beginning of wisdom. When we follow God with a sense of reverence and holy fear, when we don't take His advice as just another opinion, when we don't treat His words as just an option, we find wisdom. Now, "the fear of God" may sound old-fashioned, but that might be because we have lost our sense of reverence for the holy of holies. We have lost our awe at His power. Fear of God places us in a position of submission to His will, whereas Folly places us in a position of stubbornness where we want things our own way.

Are you asking God for wisdom and seeking it out with all your heart? Are you fearing God, seeking to build your life on His wisdom? The wise man built his house on the rock of Christ, but Folly will get you to substitute different building materials—ideologies and theories that will be here today and gone tomorrow. Wisdom isn't in a hurry, but when you take the time to follow her voice, you will build a life of quality, a life that others will want to walk beside.

DAY 28

_____

Describe a person who

exemplifies wisdom.

How do their choices,

attitudes, and behaviors

reflect godly wisdom?

FOLLOWING FREEDOM

———— *Natalie* ————

If the Son sets you free, you will be free indeed.

JOHN 8:36

We often think of freedom as an open road. We feel free when we're able to do whatever we want, whenever we want. It's the endless opportunities, no boundaries, "the sky is the limit" kind of thinking where *no* is never the answer. That's why when we think of following Jesus, it can sometimes feel like we won't experience freedom. However, a life with no limitations doesn't lead to freedom, but to death.

As human beings who were uniquely designed by God and for God, we were created to bring glory to His name. In other words, we were created for worship. We were created to love Him and be loved by Him. We were created to seek Him and find Him. We were created to be fully submitted, surrendered, and obedient to Him. The problem is if we aren't worshipping Him, we end up worshipping something else. Our hearts, our desires, and our devotion turn inward and chain us to sin. True freedom is only found in Jesus.

If you're reading it through the right lens, Scripture is basically a love letter from God to His people, telling us where true freedom is found. This is where we find Jesus in John 8 as He talks with some Jews who had believed Him. He tells them exactly where true freedom lies: "If you hold to my teaching," Jesus says, "you are really my disciples. Then you will know the truth, and the truth will set you free" (verses 31-32). The Jews responded in confusion, not recognizing how they could possibly be enslaved, and the same is often true with us. We think we are free because we have achieved what we consider independence to be, but we end up bound in sin that only masquerades as freedom. Jesus explains how the Son, referring to Himself, has the power to grant freedom—and it is true freedom. If the Son sets us free, then we are free indeed.

Following freedom doesn't mean resisting limitations but understanding that they are measures of protection. In John 10:10, Jesus promises a full life. Holding to His teachings doesn't put a cap on what you're able to experience and enjoy. Instead, it opens you up to a greater level of freedom than you knew was possible.

What does a life of freedom in Christ mean to you? What does your faith free you from, and what does it free you to do?

DAY 31

FOLLOWING GRACE

—— Natalie ——

He said to me, "My grace is sufficient for you, for my power is made perfect in weakness." Therefore I will boast all the more gladly about my weaknesses, so that Christ's power may rest on me.

2 CORINTHIANS 12:9

We all know what it feels like to mess up or fall short. Maybe what we're reaching for is simply beyond our ability. Maybe it's a display of carelessness. Or maybe it was an intentional act of cruelty. Whatever the case, we've all made mistakes. In a broken world, no one is perfect no matter how hard we try. Romans 3:23 says, "All have sinned and fall short of the glory of God." The good news is that when we repent and turn to God, we are met with His forgiveness and grace.

God loves us and favors us. He doesn't just extend His arm to us but extends His whole *self* toward us. All throughout Scripture, we see instances of God drawing closer and closer to His people. Grace is what fills in the gaps when we fall short, and there is no gap too wide. God's grace is endless. The tricky part comes when we give ourselves a hard time for how we should've known better or tried harder. Sometimes it's not even a sin issue, but we get hung up on how we don't measure up. When we listen to the voice of the enemy and shame ourselves for not being "enough," that's when we can practice receiving grace. Psalm 103:12 reminds us that "as far as the east is from the west, so far has he removed our transgressions from us." We are forgiven, we are free, and we are swimming in grace. It's okay to sink into it.

Paul knows how to follow grace as he decides to boast gladly in his weaknesses and the areas where he falls short. After hearing that God's power is made perfect in those exact areas, he sees through a new lens. As we continue in this journey of following Jesus, let's lean in and follow grace with that same lens. See what your life looks like when you start seeing God's power shine the brightest through the places that seem the darkest to you.

_____

Have you ever struggled

to receive grace? How

did God extend Himself

toward you in that time?

DAY 33

FOLLOWING FORGIVENESS

—— Charlotte ——

Her many sins have been forgiven—as her great love has shown.
But whoever has been forgiven little loves little.

LUKE 7:47

We have all heard the words *I'm sorry.* They might have come from someone who has hurt us with their words or actions. We may well have responded with the words, "I forgive you," and then walked away knowing that while the words of forgiveness had been spoken, the ways of forgiveness were not going to follow. Forgiveness is expensive and at times just feels unfair. Why should we follow forgiveness when we were not the ones who committed the crime? Yet when we refuse to forgive, we sign ourselves up for a life sentence in the prison of offense.

The Bible talks a lot about what it looks like to forgive. Jesus came to earth to model for all of us just how expensive it can be, but it was His forgiveness that gave us the freedom in which we now live. Let's not allow what we have been gifted to be wasted. In today's verse we read that forgiveness and love are closely linked; forgiveness is itself evidence of love.

Forgiving an offense means replacing reason with grace. The disciples struggled with forgiveness and asked Jesus for a little more explanation:

> Then Peter came to Jesus and asked, "Lord, how many times shall I forgive my brother or sister who sins against me? Up to seven times?" Jesus answered, "I tell you, not seven times, but seventy-seven times" (Matthew 18:21-22).

His answer was not what they wanted to hear. Holding on to offenses felt better to the disciples. But when we let bitterness take over our lives, we become spiritually stuck, preoccupied with a trial in which God has already ruled in favor of forgiveness.

The story of the prodigal son is the picture of how forgiveness can open a door that others can follow through. The prodigal had taken his inheritance and squandered it, yet his father was ready with open arms to forgive his son and restore him to a place of honor in the family. However, the older brother could not extend this forgiveness and so left no road on which his younger brother could travel back into a relationship with him. The father's heart allowed forgiveness to flow, yet the older brother allowed resentment to grow. Our ability to forgive is never just about us, it is about the people God wants to travel alongside us.

When we follow forgiveness, our heart is softened and our embrace is widened. Following forgiveness acknowledges that the debt is paid. Jesus has paid for their sin and ours. Free yourself today and let forgiveness lead the way.

---

*Reflect on a time when
you experienced radical
forgiveness. How did the
person who forgave you model
Christ's love toward us?*

FOLLOWING JOY

—— *Natalie* ——

*You make known to me the path of life; you will fill me with joy
in your presence, with eternal pleasures at your right hand.*

PSALM 16:11

We've talked how grace means God extending Himself toward us. There are so many times I look back on and recognize God's protection and provision. He loved me enough to take the punishment for my sin, He meets me exactly where I am, and He carries me through the hardest storms. He promises to give me grace enough to meet each day, and to be with me through it all!

That feeling of gratitude and gladness because of God's grace is what joy actually is. The original Greek defines it as "grace recognized" or "joy because of grace." Joy, as we define it today, refers to great pleasure and happiness. It doesn't quite hit the same without the grace part, does it?

Joy is not fleeting; it's linked to the awareness of God's grace. It's not dependent upon our circumstances or how we feel. I don't have joy simply because something good happened, which would mean I could lose it if something bad happened. I experience joy because I experience the grace of God.

When Hebrews 12:2 tells us that Jesus endured the cross "for the joy set before him," it means He endured the cross for grace, for God to be able to lean in closer to His children, and for the sheer gladness that that connection would bring Him and His people. Now, as we face challenges and trials that come our way, we can lean into and follow joy. Even if the circumstances around us don't look good, we always have something to rejoice and give thanks for because of what Jesus did on the cross. When we step into His presence and remain in Him, our joy is made complete.

DAY 36

Reflect on a time when you experienced overwhelming joy despite tough circumstances. How was God present with you in that moment?

FOLLOWING HOPE

—— *Natalie* ——

*Hope does not put us to shame, because God's love has been poured out
into our hearts through the Holy Spirit, who has been given to us.*

ROMANS 5:5

Hope. We hear the word all the time in statements like "I hope you can come" or "I hope it works out for you." This version of hope sounds nice, but it's a reflection of wishful thinking and isn't necessarily something we can take to the bank. We've watered it down to simply an expression of what we'd like to see happen while also leaving room for the possibility of it not occurring. In other words, we throw the word *hope* out there where we know it belongs, but we don't stand on it. Instead, we hold it at arm's length, distancing ourselves from the potential pain and disappointment we might feel if circumstances don't turn out the way we wanted.

Whenever we're waiting for something we believe will happen, we're standing in the gap between what we can see and what's to come. Hope is what stretches between us and carries us to where we believe we're going, but the thing is, "hope that is seen is no hope at all" (Romans 8:24). By definition, hope is something we can't see, and only God knows where we will end up if we take a step out in faith.

It can be a bit risky to step out in faith and follow hope. I'm familiar with the heartbreak, disappointment, and pain that comes when I step out and end up in a place I never thought I'd be. It makes me want to lean away rather than lean in, but Romans 5:3-4 encourages us that we can rejoice in the trials because it develops endurance, and endurance develops strong character, and strong character leads to a confident hope. It can be tempting to want to keep your distance and "hope" it ends well, but hope is meant to be firm and secure, like an anchor (Hebrews 6:19). It's meant for us to stand confidently in the gap between where we are and where we're going and speak with bold expectation that what God has promised will come to pass.

When we follow hope, the path may not look attractive and it certainly won't be easy, but we can be sure that God is with us, filling us with His love and encouraging us. And we are able to get our hopes up because *this hope* does not lead to disappointment.

What do you hope for? What promises of God can you rest on as you stand in the gap between what you see and what will come?

FOLLOWING KINDNESS

—— *Charlotte* ——

He took out two denarii and gave them to the innkeeper.
"Look after him," he said, "and when I return, I will
reimburse you for any extra expense you may have."

LUKE 10:35

Kindness is a magnet. When people are kind, their words and attitude draw you in. Kindness is an attractive way to walk and might seem like something that would be easy to follow. Yet often kindness is costly, requiring thoughtfulness and intentionality. The kind gesture needs time and investment; the kind words need to be deliberated before they are delivered. As good as the path of kindness is, the truth is that often we just don't want to take the time to walk down it.

The story of the Good Samaritan shows us three men all walking down the same road, all with places to go and responsibilities to take care of. Only one would choose to follow the path of kindness and cross the road. The Samaritan's kindness cost him his time, his attention, and, as we see in today's verse, his money. This kindness was all about benefiting a stranger with no guarantee of anything in return. Kindness is so often expressed in our small circle: We are kind to those who we think will be kind in return. Yet kindness wants us to cross the street to the lives of people who may never thank us or show kindness back to us.

We can all recall moments of sincere kindness. These moments change us; they are significant. When you show that sort of kindness to others, it's not about you. It's about others seeing the goodness and kindness of God through you. Those actions leave a mark on people's lives. Kindness called down Zacchaeus from the tree and sent Jesus to his house for dinner, transforming his position in the community in which he lived. Kindness prompted a young boy to offer his lunch to Jesus and set the scene for a miracle we are still learning from today.

In 2 Samuel, we read of the kindness of King David to a man called Mephibosheth, a man who had lived a life of brokenness and pain. David asked, "Is there anyone still left of the house of Saul to whom I can show kindness for Jonathan's sake?" (2 Samuel 9:1).

David deliberately set out to show kindness. He found out about Mephibosheth and his kindness went into action. Kindness invited a man who was broken to come to the king's table. Kindness carried him in and clothed him and allowed him to reclaim his name.

Our kindness can do the same. The adventure your heart needs may happen when kindness causes you to cross the street.

Recall a time when you

experienced the unmerited

kindness of another person.

What motivated the other

person, and how were

you moved to respond?

PART THREE

DARE
TO
UNFOLLOW

UNFOLLOWING IN A "FOLLOW ME" GENERATION

—— *Charlotte* ——

*The time will come when people will not put up with sound doctrine.
Instead, to suit their own desires, they will gather around them a
great number of teachers to say what their itching ears want to hear.*

2 TIMOTHY 4:3

I am not a very technical person. Let me rephrase that: I am terrible with technology. So when it came to starting an Instagram account, I quickly became overwhelmed by all the people I could follow. From fashion brands to ministries, friends near and far away, suddenly everyone was saying, "Hey, follow me!" With a click of a button, I had agreed to do just that. It wasn't long before I realized that following so many accounts was exhausting. I had information overload and now a dilemma: How could I unfollow without feeling I was breaking some unspoken agreement? The ease with which I started following was now starkly contrasted by the awkwardness I felt in unfollowing.

I think our lives can often feel this same way. We are the "follow me" generation with so many options of who to follow, so many opinions that want our attention. We can quickly get involved in a vast array of conversations and even when we get overwhelmed, we still feel we have to follow more to know more. So how do we resist the peer pressure and unfollow, leave the discussion that we know is bringing division, detach from the voices telling us to change? How do we unfollow someone we've given a space in our lives that we now want to take back?

If we really want to follow the right voice, then we need to unfollow the noise. Our verse today tells us that people will follow whatever their "itching ears" want to hear. The instruction God's people are given, by contrast, is to keep our heads on straight, stay focused, and not get distracted.

When you learn to drive, the only voice to listen to is your instructor: Turn off the radio, don't get caught up in a conversation with someone in the back, turn the phone to silent, and focus on the teacher's instructions. Now apply this to the voices in your life: What seemed harmless background noise at first has become hazardous to your journey. When is it time to get your eyes back on the road that you're called to?

When Jesus called His disciples, He said two words: *follow Me.* In those two words, they were given a challenge. To follow Him, they would have to unfollow everything else. They had to shift priorities; they changed vocation, location, and destination because following Jesus started a whole new way of living. Today, maybe the quickest way to clarify your following of Christ is to start unfollowing the other things that are taking your attention.

Who have you been following? What's taking up space and getting more attention than it deserves in your life? What would silencing the noise make room for in your life?

UNFOLLOW YOUR FEAR

—— *Natalie* ——

Peace I leave with you; my peace I give you. I do not give to you as the world gives. Do not let your hearts be troubled and do not be afraid.

JOHN 14:27

Jesus tells us in John 16 that we will have trouble in this world. Too often, we breeze over this statement to the more cheerful part: "Take heart! I have overcome the world" (John 16:33). The peace and victory of Jesus is an incredible gift that brings unshakable confidence and hope in the midst of any circumstance. That is something we should stand on, but let's take a minute to really think about what Jesus is saying. He has it covered, but there *will* be trouble. We *will* find ourselves in situations we can't see the way out of, and we won't be exempt from the pressure we feel from the circumstances that surround us. It's when we're in the midst of those situations that we feel afraid, confused, or stuck. We tend to wonder if we did something wrong or if God has left us, and we're tempted to follow fear because we think it will lead us back to a safer place. But *take heart.* Jesus said this would happen, and He also said we don't have to be afraid when it does.

Unfollowing fear doesn't mean you avoid fear; it means that you don't let it drive the car. Fear is a valuable survival mechanism that helps us recognize danger. But even when you sense fear, you don't have to let it overtake you.

> Do not fear, for I am with you; do not be dismayed, for I am your God. I will strengthen you and help you; I will uphold you with my righteous right hand (Isaiah 41:10).

As we find ourselves in a wide range of situations, fear will try to dictate the decisions we make. It will tell us we need to play it safe or have a backup plan in case God doesn't come through on His promise. What we need to remember is that God never goes back on His word. If He said it, He will do it.

When you unfollow fear and follow Jesus, you gain unrestricted access to His peace. That peace that surpasses all understanding and guards our hearts and minds. The world will give you trouble, but Jesus fills your heart with peace.

Describe a time when fear threatened to overwhelm you. How did you encounter God's peace in the midst of your fear?

UNFOLLOW YOUR PRIDE

—— *Natalie* ——

Humble yourselves before the Lord, and he will lift you up.

JAMES 4:10

It's the "what if" questions that stop me. Perhaps you've noticed those springing up in your own mind. *What if people think I'm weird? What if it wasn't really the voice of God? What if no one else understands?* There are a million scenarios that can make us pause rather than immediately obey and lean in closer to Jesus, and they all stem from our own pride. We want to look or be perceived a certain way. We want to keep our name, our image, our status. We want to preserve what we've built so we can use it later. It's an uncomfortable feeling to have nothing in our hands or nothing to our name. But that's how it is in the kingdom of God. It's not about our name, but His. To God be the glory, not to me.

Unfollowing pride means laying it all down. There is nothing you won't do because there is nothing preventing you from doing it. In other words, you have nothing to lose. It's the ultimate "Here am I; send me" statement (Isaiah 6:8).

It doesn't feel great to my flesh to be in that position, but it's the perfect posture to be in for God to move. And when the Lord moves, nothing can stop what He has set out to accomplish. He takes what feels like nothing and turns it into everything.

Before David was king, he was a shepherd. The youngest of his father's sons, he was not even considered worthy to be included when Samuel came to meet with them, yet God chose him to be king. God chose to make his name great and to establish his house. He wasn't perfect, but when he made mistakes, he owned them. When he recognized he had sinned, he repented. David's goal was never to exalt his own name or to preserve his own image. God saw his heart, and He drew near to it, bestowing honor on David.

Pride cannot gain a foothold when we operate from a place of humility, just like David did. But as fallen sinners, it inevitably does and we need to go back to God and ask for forgiveness. Pride strives to save face at all costs but Jesus sees behind the mask behind which we desperately hide and offers Himself, lifting us up out of the shame that pride cannot abide.

What is your point of greatest pride? Is there any way in which this pride keeps you from depending on God?

DAY 47

UNFOLLOW STRIVING

—— *Charlotte* ——

*I have promised to bring you up out of your misery in Egypt
into the land of the Canaanites, Hittites, Amorites, Perizzites,
Hivites and Jebusites—a land flowing with milk and honey.*

EXODUS 3:17

There's a fine line we can walk between pursuing our dreams and striving to make them happen. We can move from trusting to pushing, from letting God make a way to forcing our own way. We can disguise our striving as "helping God out," moving things forward on His behalf... and yet so often, when we strive, we live at a pace we cannot sustain. What we force open, we have to keep forcing to stay open.

God's plan is that our life would find a flow, yet so often we prefer to strive because it gives us a greater sense of control. Often, our striving is a sign of spiritual immaturity. We're impatient, wanting whatever we seek *now*. What we force and what God endorses are both available to our lives; we can follow the pathway of striving, or we can allow our lives to follow the flow that is only found in surrender, waiting for what God has predestined before time began. It would seem such an obvious choice to follow God's way, but we are so used to the striving culture around us, saying yes to the life of slow seems harder than saying yes to striving stress.

The children of Israel were forced into a life of captivity, cruelty, and labor by their Egyptian owners. God saw their plight and sent them deliverance in the form of Moses. Yet the Bible tells us that even after their miraculous escape from Egypt, they didn't trust God with their future. They made their own gods, trying to shape their destinies with their own hands. Their unwillingness to trust meant they signed a death warrant over their future, and that generation died in a wilderness of lack outside the doorway to a land of plenty.

We too often romanticize the past. The children of Israel reminisced about the meals they had eaten back in Egypt, forgetting the chains they had been in. Sometimes we would rather eat the meal we have strived to produce than eat from the table that we have to trust in to taste.

We all have places in our lives where we know we can force the future or we can follow the Father. If you're standing at the crossroads of striving and trusting, consider the destinations. One leads to captivity, the other to freedom. Today, examine where striving may be disguising itself and choose to stop forcing what God is not endorsing.

What have you been striving after? Are there any doors you're trying to force open? Imagine how it would feel to release that pressure on yourself and wait for God to move.

UNFOLLOW SELF

—— *Natalie* ——

*Jesus said to his disciples, "Whoever wants to be my disciple must
deny themselves and take up their cross and follow me."*

MATTHEW 16:24

I don't know about you, but I have opinions about which way is the right way to do things or move forward toward a certain goal. I gather information and map it out based on what I think will not only be the best for me but also bring the most glory to God. I aim to be thoughtful and kind about it, especially when someone else comes along and shares a differing opinion. I'm open to listening, but depending on what it is, I can sometimes nod my head with a smile but still think I'm right.

This can translate over into what I read in Scripture or hear from God throughout the day. He often challenges my line of thought with a different way of thinking, and if I'm not careful, I can hear what He says but continue along the path I have decided in my heart is the right way. I'm grateful for the conviction of the Holy Spirit, who gently and kindly speaks straight to my heart.

Recognizing you got it wrong, laying down your pride, and changing directions can all feel uncomfortable. But it's equally uncomfortable to follow down another path God has not ordained. The question we always want to ask is, How can I know that *this* path is going to be the best one for *me?* But Jesus tells His disciples to lay it all down in Matthew 16. If we want to follow Him, we must deny ourselves. First Peter 5:7 tells us to cast all our thoughts, opinions, plans, and emotions on Jesus because He cares for us. He wants us to open our hands and lay it all at His feet. He wants us to trust Him with our cares and not be limited by our own capacity.

If we want to truly follow Jesus, we have to make room for what He has for us. Sometimes that means we don't know the plan. Other times it means we know some of the plan, but we don't understand how it will ultimately shake out. Either way, He is worthy to be trusted with our whole selves. We can only go where He wants to take us if we let go of our own thoughts, plans, and will.

Are you ever tempted to lean on your own way of thinking instead of trusting God's path? Reflect on a time when God redirected you. Where did this new path lead you?

UNFOLLOW YOUR PAST

—— *Charlotte* ——

*One thing I do: Forgetting what is behind and straining toward
what is ahead, I press on toward the goal to win the prize for
which God has called me heavenward in Christ Jesus.*

PHILIPPIANS 3:13-14

Has anyone ever hurt you? Yep, me too. Maybe also like me, your first thought is probably not to forgive and move on but instead to hold on a little too long to that hurt. When we are wronged, we feel so misunderstood that to somehow simply leave that pain in the past seems a foolish, even a wrong thing to do. After all, what about my side of the story? But holding on to the past can keep us from moving toward the future.

When we allow past hurts and disappointments to remain in our lives, they become more than an unpleasant memory. They take up residence. Your past wants to feed off your future by keeping you angry and bitter. When we look at the life of Joseph, we can see plenty of hurt in his past he could have felt bitter about. His brothers abandoned him, he was falsely accused by Potiphar's wife, he was put in prison for a crime he didn't commit. Joseph had to make a choice: He could sit in his cell and plot revenge, or he could sit in his cell and release those who had wronged him. Joseph chose the latter: He didn't try to prove his innocence. Instead, he chose to act faithfully and wait for God to prove Himself.

Joseph refused to let the pain of his past share his cell, and when he left that jail he didn't take the prison bars with him. When he opened his mouth, instead of anger, he spoke with maturity…and he got the attention of the king.

The ultimate picture of how Joseph unfollowed his past was that when he finally had the opportunity to hurt the ones who hurt him, he blessed them instead. We need to recognize where bitterness has become the barrier to the blessing that forgiveness brings.

We can't change what has happened in the past, but we can decide what will flow through us. Every offense is an opportunity for demotion or promotion. If we remain in the past then the offense will have the best of us, but if we are fixed on Jesus, offense has no hold on us. I don't know who hurt you, but I do know you should give it into the hands of God who sees it all, who sees what we reap and what we sow. Isn't your future more important than the holding cell of your past? Shed the weight that has been holding you down and soar into all God has in store for you.

What past bitterness have you brought into your present? What would releasing it mean for your future—and the future of the person who hurt you?

UNFOLLOW FOMO

—— *Natalie* ——

*"My son," the father said, "you are always with
me, and everything I have is yours."*

LUKE 15:31

We've all experienced the fear of missing out. It creeps in when we've been invited somewhere fun or offered an incredible opportunity that didn't fit our schedule or just didn't pan out. It comes when we've made a tentative commitment but tried to leave the calendar open-ended in case something better comes along. We're always wondering what we could have had, or what we almost had but didn't. To make matters worse, photos and videos boasting about an event you missed fill your social media feed. The feeling of missing out—whether on a social event or an opportunity to advance your career—tends to leave us on high alert for what might be coming our way. We keep our eyes peeled, looking to the left and to the right in search of all good things so we won't miss out. But the truth is, when we follow Jesus, we never miss out.

In the parable of the lost son, the younger son wants his share of his father's estate sooner because he's convinced there's more out there for him than what he has. Riddled with the fear of missing out, he takes everything he has and ends up losing it all in the pursuit of what seems like "more." He eventually returns home to a father who is so thrilled to have him back that he throws a party. The love and forgiveness the father extends to his son who acted so foolishly is certainly worth coming back to time and time again. However, how the father responds to his older son is equally as remarkable.

The older son didn't see the world and think he was missing out. No, he saw the love of his father for his brother and thought he was missing out. Sometimes we make all the right choices, but the fear of missing out still sneaks its way in. The father responds by pointing out that the younger son isn't getting anything more than what the older son already has. "Everything I have is yours," he says.

Jesus says the same thing to us. Everything He has is ours, but are we receiving it? When we choose to follow Him, we don't have to worry about what we might be missing out on. His hand always leads away from what will destroy us and into an abundant, full life.

What have you been worried about missing out on? How have you seen God providing for you and protecting you when He says no?

UNFOLLOW RELIGIOUS RULES

—— *Natalie* ——

People are counted as righteous, not because of their work,
but because of their faith in God who forgives sinners.

ROMANS 4:5 NLT

When you're in a relationship with someone, you don't need to follow a list of rules in order to be friends with them. The way you talk to them, spend time with them, and get to know them isn't something you can map out; it's something you have to figure out. Likewise, following Jesus means going deeper and entering into a personal relationship with Him.

Religious rules can sometimes restrict us from being fully engaged with Jesus. We may check off the boxes of going to church and reading Scripture, but what we do in our own strength puts us in a position to be working for something rather than freely receiving it. Romans 4 reminds us that it's not by what we do that brings us into salvation, but the grace of Jesus alone. The focus is on Him, what He has done for us, and how He meets us exactly where we are to bring us where we need to go. We get to let ourselves fully sink into who He is. The veil has been torn for a reason; we get to go all the way in!

> I no longer call you servants, because a servant does not know his master's business. Instead, I have called you friends, for everything that I learned from my Father I have made known to you (John 15:15).

We aren't mindless workers, following instructions instead of knowing the Master's business. Jesus has called us friends and given us full access to the Father through Him. First Corinthians 2:16 tells us we have the mind of Christ. We can know His thoughts and His plans, but like any relationship, we have to enter in and engage with Him. We have to spend time with Him, talk to Him, and learn who He is so that when He reveals things to us, we understand them in the context of who He is. As we continue to follow Jesus, let's unfollow the rules that try to tell us the "right" way to do it and just go all the way in with Him!

Have religious rules or the "right" way to approach God been helpful or harmful in your walk with Him? How do you best engage with Jesus?

UNFOLLOW THE CROWD

—— *Charlotte* ——

When he heard that it was Jesus of Nazareth, he began to shout, "Jesus, Son of David, have mercy on me!" Many rebuked him and told him to be quiet, but he shouted all the more, "Son of David, have mercy on me!"

MARK 10:47-48

Jesus spent His life surrounded by crowds. For three years of public ministry He taught, healed, ministered, and showed compassion to the crowds that followed Him. Yet that same crowd also rejected Him, shouting, "Crucify him!" Jesus knew the crowd was fickle; He was no people pleaser who built His ministry around their demands. He didn't follow the crowd or allow them to define what He was called to do. Jesus was the same with one as He was with thousands. He showed His disciples that the pull of the crowd should never detract their focus from the calling, that His followers should never be swayed by popular opinion.

Where in your life does the crowd have too much control? What movement is asking you to follow, what noise is overwhelming your senses, what pressure is swaying your ability to obey? We read in the Bible of a blind beggar named Bartimaeus who had been ignored and rebuked by the crowd all his life. The day Jesus was in the neighborhood, Bartimaeus decided he was tired of the crowd telling him how to behave. He began shouting for Jesus and the crowd, as usual, told him to be quiet. Yet this day was different. Bartimaeus wasn't going to follow the crowd, he was not going to stay silent. He was going to shout for Jesus.

Sometimes you have to raise your voice in order to unfollow the crowd. You have to be willing to be unpopular. The crowd was keeping Bartimaeus from his miracle, and the crowd can do the same to you. Would you rather keep your crowd happy and stay blind, or leave the crowd behind and shout to Jesus? That day, Bartimaeus left the crowd, and he had the opportunity to be face-to-face with Jesus, to be asked by the Son of God what he wanted. If Bartimaeus had allowed the crowd to shut him down, if he had followed their lead, he would never have asked the question or received the answer that transformed him.

Don't be desperate to please the crowd that has no real commitment to you. Look at how fickle the crowd was: When Jesus spoke to Bartimaeus, they switched sides and called to him too. But Bartimaeus no longer needed to get their permission. Instead, he was following Jesus. At that moment, he was given the miracle of restored sight. Perhaps today, his story can encourage you to do the same, to leave the crowd and, instead, call out to Jesus.

What is it you need to bring

to Jesus that the crowd is

trying to silence within you?

UNFOLLOW THE LIE

—— *Charlotte* ——

Jesus answered, "I am the way and the truth and the life.
No one comes to the Father except through me."

JOHN 14:6

I don't think any of us deliberately decide to follow a lie. However, often lies are well disguised and parade themselves as truths we should not just follow but actively pursue. The more we follow that lie, the more we believe it, and the more it begins to shape who we become.

Remember the story of the ugly duckling? It believed it was ugly, its reflection showed that it wasn't beautiful enough to fit in with all the others. The lie sent the duckling into hiding, living isolated in a world of insecurity. The ugly duckling had believed it was something it was not—it was actually a beautiful swan, waiting for release from the lie it had been living.

Our own lives can mirror this story. We can accept the lie we are told by a jealous friend, believe it when we are told we are worthless by someone who has no care for our future. We can allow careless, untrue words to define us.

The lies we follow become the prison we volunteer for. The father of lies will manufacture so many lies about your identity and your worth. The more lies we digest, the sicker we become, and that's why we have to unfollow the lie and follow the truth. What does Jesus say about you? His truth says you are fearfully and wonderfully made (Psalm 139:14); His truth says you are the head and not the tail (Deuteronomy 28:13); His truth says He loves you with an everlasting love (Jeremiah 31:3).

It's hard to trust again when so many have broken that trust, but we can't allow people's frailty to overshadow God's sovereignty. If you've believed a lie about your value, then read the truth where God speaks of how He loves and even sings over you (Zephaniah 3:17). If it's a lie about your past, then read the truth about how He has forgiven you and removed your sins as far as the east is from the west (Psalm 103:12). If the lie is that you have no future, then read the truth about the One who has already ordained your days (Psalm 139:16).

Follow the truth because the truth sets you free. If you don't feel free in any area, examine what you believe. Lies make us feel restricted but the truth brings a sense of liberty. Today, read truth, speak truth, and follow truth. You will find that the truth will lead you right past the place where the lie was trying to keep and control you.

What lies have you

accepted about your

worth and value?

How could you replace

those lies with the truth

of God's Word?

PART FOUR

DARE TO LEAD FROM A PLACE OF FOLLOWING

FOLLOW ME AS I FOLLOW CHRIST

—— *Charlotte* ——

Follow my example, as I follow the example of Christ.

1 CORINTHIANS 11:1

Have you ever taken the lead in a convoy of vehicles, assuring them if they follow you, they will be heading in the right direction? Perhaps you've been the one trying to get everyone to the right place at the right time and as you follow Google Maps, you are desperately hoping it is taking you exactly where you all need to go. The pressure to lead means you need to know the source you are following is good, that it's going to guide you to where the whole group needs to go.

We can often forget that every day, people are following our lives. This can be in our immediate circle—family and close friends who we regularly do life with—or in a wider circle of people we work with, members of our church, or perhaps people we teach. It may be people we have never met who are following us; more than ever, our lives are open to follow through the influence we have on social media. These people—those close to us and those in a totally different world—are watching how we navigate the situations that arise in all our lives.

Following is more prevalent than ever and yet as we look around, we see more people lost and confused. That's why it's so important, as people follow our lives, that we check who we are following. We are being affected not just by what we see but also by what they are seeing. The lens through which they view life is shaping the path they are leading us on. We can follow someone who says they follow Jesus, and yet find we end up on a pathway that doesn't feel or reflect the ways or words of our Savior. You can't follow Jesus and also follow your offense. You can't follow Jesus and also follow your pride. Whichever has the greatest pull will be what the people following behind you will eventually feel.

We are all leading someone, so don't wait for a platform or a position to work on your leading ability. Decide today to be aware afresh of those around you now and become a better leader by devoting yourself to being a greater follower. If we follow His ways, we will lead people in them. If we follow His heart, we will model that to others. The confidence to invite people to follow you comes from the certainty of the source in front of you. Grow in your knowledge of the One who leads you by still waters, who leads you through the valleys, even through enemy territory. When our GPS is God, then our leading will be good and we can confidently say, like Paul, *you can follow me as I follow Christ*.

———————————

Today, in whatever activities you have planned, how can you model the heart of Jesus to the people around you?

FOLLOWING IN FRIENDSHIP

—— *Charlotte* ——

I no longer call you servants, because a servant does not know his master's business. Instead, I have called you friends, for everything that I learned from My Father I have made known to you.

JOHN 15:15

One of the greatest sources of joy in life is found in the journey of friendship. Friendship is not just a good idea, it's a God idea. God doesn't want us to do life alone; He wants us to find a community, to build a life where our friendships flourish. Jesus was known as the friend of sinners, which means we all qualify to be His friend. So how often do you really lean into Jesus as your friend? How can His example help you become a better friend?

Jesus teaches us to forgive quickly, how to be more patient and understanding. Following Jesus in our friendships means we can learn to avoid the pathways of division and animosity and start to learn the ways of peace and unity.

I have been blessed with some incredible friendships in my life. One of those friends is writing this book with me. As Nat and I have journeyed the years together, I am so mindful of the glue that has held our friendship together. Jesus has been central to our relationship from the very beginning—He is the reason we found each other, and He is the common ground we chose to build on together.

The foundation a friendship is built on is so important. If we build on joint interests and hobbies alone, we will find the foundations are too shallow to handle storms. When a friendship is founded on Christ, however, we discover that in places of adversity, what could have fallen apart finds a new tenacity. Remember in Daniel 3 when the three friends—Shadrach, Meshach, and Abednego—ended up in a furnace? They found that a fourth friend joined them. Jesus was that friend; He held them as friends in the fire and He will do the same for you in your friendships.

I want to encourage you in the areas of your life where you have friendships entrusted to you. Grow those friendships by following the example of Jesus. He was a friend to His disciples. He didn't just teach them—He loved them, He cared for them, He stood by them. He even loved them when they betrayed Him, doubted Him, and denied Him. By following this example, we can become a better friend to those who have extended to us the privilege of this beautiful relationship. Today, put Jesus in the middle of every relationship and you will find that a three-cord strand is not easily broken.

Reflect on a friendship in which you've felt God's guidance, presence, and comfort. How could you invite Jesus further into that relationship?

FOLLOWING IN MY FAMILY

—— *Natalie* ——

I assure you that everyone who has given up house or brothers or sisters or mother or father or children or property, for my sake and for the Good News, will receive now in return a hundred times as many houses, brothers, sisters, mothers, children, and property—along with persecution. And in the world to come that person will have eternal life.

MARK 10:29-30 NLT

When you've lived away from home for a while, going back to visit for holidays or family gatherings can be a tricky experience to navigate. As you've spent time apart from your family and their influence on your life and your choices, you've likely learned and grown in ways they haven't seen or been part of. Returning home to the people who have known you the longest and are familiar with who you once were can be challenging. Either there is a bit of tension caused by a new dynamic, or you end up reverting back to old patterns and letting the atmosphere dictate your words and actions. Even Jesus faced this struggle when He returned to His hometown after beginning His ministry, and we are no exception.

Following Jesus involves a personal relationship with Him that enables us to walk in true freedom as daughters of the King. No matter how close you might be to your family, they're not in your relationship with God and they don't hear from Him the same way you do. He has a unique relationship with all His children. It's crucial to keep this first and not allow others to dictate our behavior because of who they say we are. We must continue to live from the place of freedom, knowing who God says we are and trusting in Him.

Sometimes standing firm in your faith and remaining steadfast in following Jesus looks like tension and loss, as Jesus describes in Mark 10:29, but we are called to follow Him first. Whatever it costs, following Jesus means choosing Him over anything else, without compromise. When we do that, the fruit we bear in our lives from remaining in Him will bring glory to God and will be a powerful testimony that will draw others in. It might look backwards and feel confusing, but we pave the way for others to follow by remaining relentless in our pursuit of Jesus.

How did your family of origin show you the love of God? Were there any patterns or family dynamics that kept you from operating in the fullness of His love?

FOLLOWING IN MY COMMUNITY

—— Natalie ——

Let your light shine before others, that they may see your good deeds and glorify your Father in heaven.

MATTHEW 5:16

We each have our own sphere of influence. We often think we need a large following on social media or a platform and a microphone to really make a difference, but the truth is, we all have people around us who are listening to what we say and watching what we do. Whether we have thousands of followers, a handful of friends, or even just our immediate family, we have an opportunity to be intentional with the community we do have. We're called to let the light of Christ in us shine before others, no matter how many there are to see it.

In Genesis 40, we read about how Joseph is in prison and watching over Pharaoh's chief cupbearer and chief baker who were thrown into prison with him. While they were in prison together, Pharaoh's men each had a dream that, through God's power, Joseph was able to interpret for them. Rather than thinking little of himself as a man in prison without influence, Joseph was bold in his God-given ability and willing to share what God had revealed to him. Even though no one else was around to witness God using him, Joseph remained true to what the Lord led him to do. It took years, and probably much longer than he'd hoped, but God faithfully brought him out of prison and put him in a position of greater influence. What started with two men in prison listening to what God had to say through him turned into everyone in the land of Egypt being blessed by Joseph's God-given wisdom.

When we are faithful to shine the light of Christ to even the smallest audience, God will use it and honor it. The chief cupbearer, who promised to remember Joseph once he got out of prison, actually forgot about him for two full years. But Joseph's impact on him remained, and when Pharaoh had a couple of disturbing dreams that he needed someone to interpret, the chief cupbearer finally remembered Joseph and his ability.

It might not seem like we are making much of a difference as we continue to boldly follow Jesus in our own community, but you never know how deep the seed is planted. It may take years, but we will always reap a harvest from the seed we sow.

Who shines the brightest light in your community? In what dark space do you feel God's call to shine the light of Christ?

FOLLOWING IN MY EXAMPLE

—— *Natalie* ——

Don't let anyone think less of you because you are young. Be an example to all believers in what you say, in the way you live, in your love, your faith, and your purity.

1 TIMOTHY 4:12 NLT

I think we've all been told at one point or another to "be an example" to those around us. Being an example is just another way of saying *leadership*. We have people who are watching us and learning about how to behave based on what we choose to do, and we shouldn't take that responsibility lightly. To be an example means to set the standard or create the mold for how things should be done so others can follow suit. More often than not, when we're following Jesus, the example we set isn't what the obvious or easiest choice might be.

Scripture is full of messages that convict us to not simply do what makes sense but to act on a counterintuitive level. Turn the other cheek, rejoice in suffering, go a second mile, love your neighbor as yourself, love your enemies, pray for those who persecute you. In Matthew 5, Jesus drives this point home. He says,

> If you love those who love you, what reward will you get? Are not even the tax collectors doing that? And if you greet only your own people, what are you doing more than others? Do not even pagans do that? (verses 46-47).

It's not enough to simply do what others around us are doing. We don't lower our standards to match theirs, we show them there's a higher way. When we follow Jesus, we must use Him as our standard. In our own strength, it seems impossible and exhausting. But Isaiah 40:31 says, "Those who hope in the LORD will renew their strength. They will soar on wings like eagles; they will run and not grow weary, they will walk and not be faint." Jesus frees us from the chains of our sin so we don't have to walk in those ways anymore. We are free and empowered to be like Him. When we choose to follow Jesus and be an example of what He has done and what He is doing in our lives, we encourage others to follow Him.

Reflect on a situation in your life that would be easy to coast through. How is Jesus calling you to be like Him? What would it look like to take leadership in this circumstance?

FOLLOWING IN MY SPEECH

Natalie

The tongue has the power of life and death, and those who love it will eat its fruit.

PROVERBS 18:21

God spoke everything into existence, Jesus tells us we can move mountains with our words, and sprinkled throughout Scripture are passages that let us know how much our speech influences our lives and others. When Moses led the Israelites out of Egypt, we hear how incessantly they complained about their situation. Time and time again, they doubted God's faithfulness and spoke literal words of death over their situation. In spite of how they had experienced the miraculous power of God working on their behalf, they declared over and over that God had brought them into the wilderness just to let them die. In Numbers 14, God responds. He has heard their complaints so many times that He will do exactly what He has heard them say. He still fulfilled His promise of bringing His people into the land He had given them, but the generation who spoke death over their situation didn't get to go.

The fate of the Israelites matched their words, and they died in the wilderness. On the flip side, speaking life also brings life. Romans 10:9 tells us, "If you declare with your mouth, 'Jesus is Lord,' and believe in your heart that God raised him from the dead, you will be saved." As followers of Jesus, we must both believe *and declare*. "For it is with your heart that you believe and are justified, and it is with your mouth that you profess your faith and are saved" (verse 10). Speaking what's true, and not just believing it, is what moves mountains.

We all have the power to shift our situation by how we speak about it, but it's not just to our own benefit when we choose to speak life instead of death. Just like the worship of Paul and Silas broke the chains of everyone in prison with them in Acts 16, the true and good promises of God that you steep your situation in will break the chains of those around you who are listening. Showing others the way of Jesus doesn't always come by speaking directly about Him; sometimes it comes by the way you speak about your situation through the lens of His truth, even if the circumstances don't look good. The hope and joy and life you experience when you trust God overflows to those around you when you choose to speak the truth of God.

Reflect on a friend who seems bound by chains of doubt, uncertainty, or pain. How could God use you to speak of His victory and power over those chains?

FOLLOWING IN MY ACTION

—— *Natalie* ——

Do you see that faith was working together with his works,
and by works faith was made perfect?

JAMES 2:22 NKJV

When we're going through a difficult situation, people will often try to encourage us by reminding us to trust God and have faith. Unfortunately, in the midst of challenging situations, statements like that can feel like just words. We can *know* God is good and faithful and never lets us down, but it doesn't always *feel* like it. Our experience doesn't match what we've heard, and it causes us to pause or doubt or question God. But faith comes alive when we put action to our words.

In the book of Acts, we read that early Christians were called followers of "the Way." I love this term because it not only speaks to who Jesus is but to how believers follow Him. Too often, we can get caught up in the routine of Christianity and forget that we are followers of the Way too. It's not just about what we believe or what we say, it's about what we do. Believing the truth, and even speaking the truth, doesn't carry much weight unless you follow it through with action. If you believe God is your provider, for example, then an act of faith might look like being generous when it feels like you're in lack or taking the job He's leading you into that comes with a smaller salary. We don't just tell the people around us what we believe, we show them.

> Make it your goal to live a quiet life, minding your own business and working with your hands, just as we instructed you before. Then people who are not believers will respect the way you live, and you will not need to depend on others (1 Thessalonians 4:11-12 NLT).

The people around us should be able to look at our lives and see what we believe without our having to spell it out for them. Whether or not they believe the same things we do, there will be no question about where we put our trust. When you're following in the way of Jesus, you will always find your way to the Father, and anyone watching will see the way too.

How is God prompting you to show your belief in Him? If you trust that God will protect, provide, and care for you, what would it look like to demonstrate that trust?

FOLLOWING IN MY REACTIONS

—— *Charlotte* ——

When Jesus' followers saw what was going to happen, they said, "Lord, should we strike with our swords?" And one of them struck the servant of the high priest, cutting off his right ear. But Jesus answered, "No more of this!" And he touched the man's ear and healed him.

LUKE 22:49-51

Who's with me? When you hear the word *Surprise!* shouted on a special occasion, does your heart sink? I have told my husband multiple times: no surprises. Surprises are supposed to provoke certain reactions, and the excited people who plan them want a person to be delighted by the occasion. The introvert in me panics that I can't live up to their expectations.

We all have areas in our life where our reactions are not going to meet other people's expectations. Our reactions are fed by our feelings...and following feelings rarely leads us on the best path. The less we follow feelings, the more we remove the power of our reactions to make our choices.

When Jesus was arrested in the garden of Gethsemane, Peter was hurt and confused. His feelings overwhelmed him, so he grabbed his sword to defend his teacher. Jesus responded to this act of violence by healing the man who had been wounded.

Reactions can propel us down a path whose end we cannot see. If you're at a place where you're tempted to make a quick reaction, follow, instead, the example of Jesus. The Bible tells us to pray for our enemies, even give them our best coat. This might not be our natural reaction; we want to retaliate, to hurt the person who hurt us. But Jesus is giving us a new path to follow. This means we have to determine our actions ahead of our conversations.

Imagine right now if I was to throw a ball to you. Your reaction would probably be to try to catch it. But what if I told you not every ball that is thrown toward you is something you should catch? In fact, some should never get to be in your hands at all. The enemy is constantly trying to throw balls at our life to cause a reaction. He wants us catching "balls" that will distract and derail our lives. He wants our hands full of the wrong things that will prevent us from holding the right things. We have to learn to discern and follow Christ instead of reacting to the crisis.

You can't always avoid the conflict, but you can determine what your actions will be. You can control your temper and instead, follow the One who can calm the storm within you and around you.

When the enemy throws you a curveball, do you react? Or do you pause and go to God for wisdom? What tends to be the outcome of each choice?

FOLLOWING IN MY CHOICES

—— Charlotte ——

This day I call the heavens and the earth as witnesses against you that I have set before you life and death, blessings and curses. Now choose life, so that you and your children may live and that you may love the LORD your God, listen to his voice, and hold fast to him.

DEUTERONOMY 30:19-20

When the world was hit by the pandemic early in 2020, everyone's life changed. For some, the effects of what followed were devastating: Many lost their lives, people lost jobs and endured financial hardship, and families were separated for months or even years.

When the effects of the pandemic started to take hold, I was in England. Every event in my calendar was cancelled as the lockdowns took hold. The doors of our own church were closed to our church family. I felt that my life was no longer my own—everything was changing, and I had no control over my circumstances. It was then that today's verse in Deuteronomy came alive to me in a brand-new way. Though I couldn't change the circumstances, my choices would either make this season better or worse. That day, I chose to get up, grab my phone, and start recording what became a daily devotional I posted for over a year, encouraging people to choose well.

Today I Choose became a pathway for many to follow in the pandemic, but it began with one simple choice. I could choose to follow my circumstances, or I could choose to follow Christ. I wanted to choose well. I wanted to choose to believe and not doubt; choose to put faith over fear; choose to pray and not panic. In choosing to record these simple daily devotionals, I was choosing to lead people toward life, not death.

Every day we make hundreds of choices, and some have more consequences than others. Some choices will alter what comes next in your life: blessings or curses. So how aware are you of your power to choose? Perhaps right now you are feeling powerless, but I want to remind you, this power of choice has been given to you by Christ.

What will you give your energy to? What conversation will you choose to enter or exit? Who will you choose to allow to speak into your life? What will you choose to speak into the lives of others, no matter the situation? All these choices belong to you. In a prison cell, Joseph could choose to get bitter or better. In a harem, Esther could choose to give up or step up. In the face of a battle, Gideon could choose to hide or lead. We all get to choose, so today, don't believe the lie of the enemy that nothing can change. Realize that God gave you the power to choose. Who you choose to follow determines what harvest you plant for the future.

_No matter what circumstance
you're facing, how will you
choose to speak life today?
What intentional choices
can you make to show
God's power over pain?_

FOLLOWING AS A LEADER

—— Charlotte ——

[Elijah] came to a broom bush, sat down under it and prayed that he might die. "I have had enough, LORD," he said. "Take my life."

1 KINGS 19:4

The privilege of leadership comes with a great responsibility and a great many demands. Leadership often makes you more aware of your followers than it does of your need to follow, yet leadership is only as great as the commitment of followership. This means as a leader, you have to be more committed to listening than you are to being the one listened to. When we start losing the signal of God's voice in our lives, every leadership decision we make becomes affected, and how we lead becomes less effective.

When Elijah was out-running chariots and leading God's people and calling down fire, everyone was amazed at his leadership. Yet in that same period, Elijah was losing his perspective. He was burned out and ended up under a tree, asking God to take his life. How can leadership be so great in one moment and then so tragic in the next? The downward spiral doesn't happen in a moment, it happens over time. We can all get exhausted and as leaders, we are always a target for the enemy. That's why we must remember that in our leadership, we have to always lean into the shadow of His wings. Leadership means that as we take on the burden God gives to us, He also says He will help carry us. When we act simply in our strength, we will always fail. But when we learn to lead reliant on His strength, we will always find a way to conquer.

We must not allow the energy of the ministry to replace intimacy with the Holy Spirit. When the signs and wonders are leading more than the still small voice of the Holy Spirit, we are in trouble. When Elijah wanted to quit, God sent an angel to remind him it wasn't that he couldn't lead, it was that he had forgotten he was not leading alone. When we feel like it's too much, we need to get back to seeing that God is more than enough.

When God sent His angel to help Elijah lead again, He began by making him eat and rest. Sometimes in our leadership, we neglect the very basic things; we are so busy feeding others, we forget to feed ourselves. We are so busy bringing water for the thirst of those around us, we don't realize we are also dehydrated spiritually. Today, whatever area of leadership you are in, learn to lean into the One who said in Matthew 11:28-30 that His burden is easy and His yoke is light. Learn how to work with Him—maybe you are working for God but not with God. When we lead as Christ leads us, we find a rhythm of grace for our lives today. I pray your leading would find a new place of refreshment as you follow the unforced rhythm of leading by God's grace.

In what area of life are you a leader? In your home, your community, your church? How can you intentionally submit to the Holy Spirit's governance and guidance in this area?

PART FIVE

DARE TO FOLLOW IN ALL SEASONS

DARE TO FOLLOW IN THE STORM

—— Natalie ——

[Jesus] replied, "You of little faith, why are you so afraid?" Then he got up and rebuked the winds and the waves, and it was completely calm.

MATTHEW 8:26

Following Jesus is quite an adventure. You experience seemingly impossible miracles that only He can do. Like Peter, when we follow Jesus, there are times when we get to (metaphorically) walk on water. But consider the setting for the story of Peter walking on water: He stepped out of the boat in the middle of the night, in the middle of a storm.

I don't know about you, but if I ever got the opportunity to walk on water, my ideal weather condition for the event would be a calm, sunny day. Any sign of a storm would have me backtracking, especially if I was out on the water as the wind and waves rolled in. It's because of the storm that the disciples can't tell that it's Jesus who is walking on the water, so Peter asks Him to confirm who He is. Jesus, of course, responds by telling Peter to come. You can read the rest of the story in Matthew 14, but the thing that gets me is how Jesus is unfazed by the storm. He doesn't tell Peter it's safer for him to stay in the boat. He doesn't calm the storm before inviting Peter out. He simply tells him to come in spite of the conditions that surround them.

Earlier, in Matthew 8, we read how the disciples were with Jesus in a boat when a storm arose. They were afraid, but Jesus was sleeping. When they woke Him up, He acted like it wasn't a big deal. He calmed the wind and the waves, and they continued on in their journey. The disciples were amazed, but Jesus acted as if His power was obvious. He called them out for having little faith the same way He calls Peter out for having little faith when he gets distracted by the storm and starts to sink.

Storms come when we follow Jesus and storms come when we don't. The difference is, when we're with Jesus and keeping our eyes on Him, as distracting and scary as the circumstances around us might seem, we can always be certain that we will not be overtaken as long as we stay focused on Jesus. As we continue on this adventure of a lifetime following Him, we don't have to worry about what storms might pop up. The circumstances that surround us never hold as much power as Jesus does. It doesn't matter if it's day or night, calm or stormy, we can be confident that He is trustworthy and faithful.

Are your circumstances

sunny or stormy today?

Does that have any effect on

your response to Jesus' call?

DAY 83

DARE TO FOLLOW IN CONFLICT

—— Charlotte ——

*If anyone will not welcome you or listen to your words,
leave that home or town and shake the dust off your feet.*

MATTHEW 10:14

How much time do we waste in conversations that lead us nowhere? We can spend hours in conflict, hours that we know will never bring a good return for the time we have invested. Conflict can be part of our everyday lives—if you are a parent, you soon learn that a childish tantrum can dominate the day unless you step in and find a way to diffuse the tension. Conflict can bring confusion, and in that confusion, we can forget to follow what is right. Instead, we start to follow *being* right, fighting for personal point scoring rather than the greater plan.

When Jesus was training His disciples, He taught them how to help people, but He also taught them how not to get held up by people. When He was sending His disciples out, He warned them that they must not allow any place of conflict to interrupt their calling. If people want to argue or object to your

182

mission, He told them, don't waste any more time defending your position. Shake the dust off your feet and move on.

I think we all need to learn at times to shake that dust off. If we allow conflict to interrupt our commitment to following Jesus, we will never make the progress that is possible. If we stop to engage in every disagreement or defend every accusation, we run the risk of being distracted from what God has actually called us to. When David went to the frontline to take bread and cheese to his brothers, his eldest brother tried to cause conflict. He taunted David and sought to ridicule him. Yet we read in 1 Samuel 17 that because David was more focused on God's glory, he found himself at the center of God's whole purpose for having him there that day.

We have to keep our perspective when we sense the pull of conflict. Whether the adversity is from friends and family or we feel conflict from people around us in a work setting, in church, in our neighborhood, no one is immune. When conflict brews, ask yourself, *What would I rather invest my time in? What will bring the greatest glory to God?*

How often do we leave Goliath standing because we get distracted fighting our brothers? How much time do we waste in futile conversations when the real call is to win the battle before us? In times of conflict, keep following the Father. Even in the face of betrayal, Jesus kept following all the way to the cross, where the ultimate victory was won.

Reflect on a time when

you engaged in conflict

unwisely. How could you have

handled the circumstances

differently? What might

a different decision have

enabled you to do?

DARE TO FOLLOW IN LOSS

—— *Natalie* ——

I am glad for your sakes that I wasn't there. You're about to be given new grounds for believing. Now let's go to him.

JOHN 11:15 MSG

In church, we sing a song with the lyrics, "You are good / You're never gonna let me down." Singing that song can feel hard when we're facing a tough loss. In times of grief or disappointment, *has* Jesus let us down? We know He is good, but we didn't expect things to play out this way. The easy thing to do would be to sit down and not sing out. But following Jesus in every season means declaring what's true in the midst of what looks like the opposite.

In John 11, we read about a man named Lazarus. Lazarus was sick, but when his sisters sent word to Jesus about the illness, He didn't immediately go to his side. Instead, He waited two days. By the time Jesus arrived, Lazarus was dead and buried. At separate times, both of his sisters protested to Jesus that if only He had been there, their brother wouldn't have died. They knew Him to be the healer—why hadn't He healed Lazarus? We know the end of the story—how

Jesus resurrects Lazarus from the dead and calls him out of the grave—but what's equally incredible about this story is what Jesus says to His disciples before-hand. Lazarus has died, He tells them. But He's glad that He wasn't there to heal him because, as The Message translation puts it, "You're about to be given new grounds for believing." Everyone believed Jesus to be the One who heals, but it was important for them to also believe Him to be the One who resurrects.

As we continue to follow Jesus in every season, we can be confident that loss never points to His abandonment. It is always an opportunity to go deeper and learn new dimensions of who He is. You might know Him to be your provider, but He wants you to know Him as your protector and defender too. You might know Him to be your best friend, but He also wants you to know Him as your Father. There is always more to who He is. Experiencing loss often feels dev-astating, but it also makes room for more of Him in your life. In spite of how empty you feel as you walk through seasons of life, there is nothing like being filled up with more of Him and His love, peace, joy, and comfort. No matter how much we lose, Jesus will never let us down.

Have you experienced a loss

that felt like abandonment?

How did Jesus show

Himself to you in a new

way through this trial?

DARE TO FOLLOW IN MISUNDERSTANDING

—— *Charlotte* ——

*Some of those present were saying indignantly to one another,
"Why this waste of perfume? It could have been sold for more
than a year's wages and the money given to the poor." And they
rebuked her harshly. "Leave her alone," said Jesus. "Why are
you bothering her? She has done a beautiful thing to me."*

MARK 14:4-6

I wonder how many heroes of faith we read about spent large parts of their life being misunderstood. It's only because we can read their whole story that their apparently crazy behavior makes sense to us today. I mean, would you think Noah was normal if he were your neighbor? Watching him, day in and day out for 50 years, go into the backyard to build a large vessel to survive a flood—which was nonsense because no one had ever heard of rain. What about Joshua, who told people to march in silence so some walls could fall down? Not the easiest battle plan to understand.

Following God can mean being misunderstood. It's not a nice feeling—we want to explain ourselves so we can be accepted and appreciated. Yet the call to follow Christ will never make sense to a person who doesn't know Him. The call to surrender can't be understood by someone who only wants to serve their own agenda. The ability to forgive is not understood by those who don't understand how much they need forgiveness.

We serve a God who is misunderstood in a culture that wants to serve and fashion its own gods. That's why we often have to release ourselves from the pressure to explain everything. Noah couldn't sufficiently explain what God had asked, so he instead focused on what he had been asked to do. He knew that when God moved, no explanation would be necessary. Joshua had to live with the questioning glances every time they circled those walls, but after day seven, those who misunderstood were standing alongside the rubble of victory.

Sometimes your zeal, passion, purpose, obedience, sacrifice, and choices will be misunderstood. Yet in it all, you have to realize there is only One who is the judge. The woman who broke an alabaster jar of expensive perfume on the feet of Jesus was judged as unworthy. Her generous act was misunderstood, and yet Jesus quieted the ones who questioned. In the midst of the complaints and criticism, He showed she was the one who understood what was most necessary in that moment. Her understanding revealed the misunderstanding of the religious leaders, and her actions continue to teach us today.

So when you feel misunderstood, remember your actions are not supposed to make sense to everyone, your choices don't have to be approved by everyone. Today, trust God's leading and stop trying to clarify in the moment what may only ever make sense with time.

Describe an event in the

past where you needed

the perspective of time to

understand God's plan. What

did you learn from that

situation that could apply to

your circumstances today?

DARE TO FOLLOW IN FAILURE

—— *Natalie* ——

Though they stumble, they will never fall, for
the LORD holds them by the hand.

PSALM 37:24 NLT

We all have an idea of what success is. We know what it looks like, feels like, and how it makes us appear to other people. It's what we reach for and hold tightly. When we fall short of that goal, we call it "failure." It can feel so disappointing to realize that after all the effort and courage we put forth, we didn't get the results we wanted. Sometimes it even feels like we've not just come to a stop, but we've moved farther from our goal than where we were originally. It can be so disheartening to move forward after taking a hit, but God is faithful even when we are not. God is strong even when we are weak. God is victorious even when we can't seem to pull it together.

We must look at our "failures" in light of Christ's victory. It might seem like we messed up or will never succeed, but all we can say is that God's full purpose in all of this hasn't been revealed. All is not lost because "we know that in all things God works for the good of those who love him, who have been called according to his purpose" (Romans 8:28). Our triumph just might look different from what we expected—it's *His* purpose, and not necessarily ours.

Jesus' disciples had all kinds of ideas about what Jesus' success might look like. In fact, they often had a difficult time understanding what Jesus was saying as He taught them because they expected a different sort of victory. When Jesus ultimately went to the cross and died, they lost all hope, thinking He had failed. Later, when Jesus was resurrected and met two disciples walking along the road to Emmaus, they told Him about their pain without even recognizing Him in their pain. "We had hoped he was the Messiah who had come to rescue Israel," they said (Luke 24:21 NLT). On all accounts, it certainly looked like Jesus had failed, and it continued to look like that for days. But this point of "failure" was actually the pathway to the most victorious rescue.

As we continue to follow Jesus in every season, we can be confident that He is turning every "failure" into an even greater success than we had envisioned. He is our victory, and no failure we experience can overpower what He has planned. Our victory is secured, and as we walk it out, He meets us exactly where we are to bring us where we need to be. We don't have to be afraid of what might not work out because He is intentional and purposeful and He will never let us fall.

What past failure can you now see as a stepping-stone to victory? What is the ultimate victory we hope for in Jesus Christ?

DARE TO FOLLOW IN DISAPPOINTMENT

—— Charlotte ——

His wife said to him, "Are you still maintaining your integrity?
Curse God and die!"
He replied, "You are talking like a foolish woman.
Shall we accept good from God, and not trouble?"

JOB 2:9-10

Overnight, Job went from living a life of luxury, surrounded by his family, to living a life of poverty and misery. His children were killed, his thriving farm was destroyed, and he was afflicted with sickness. As their life took the very worst turn of events, Job's wife decided she was finished following God, and she urged her husband to make the same declaration. But Job responded, essentially, "Should I accept good from God and not hold fast in the bad?" Job had a revelation that his decision to follow God was not based on his level of satisfaction, but on the depth of his conviction. In a world where we click "unfollow" as soon as we feel someone has let us down, this is upside-down thinking.

Disappointment is a part of life, and our ability to handle it correctly can actually enhance and even propel our lives forward. You often learn more about your conviction in a time when you feel most disappointed. It's when the friend lets you down that you discover how deep that friendship is rooted. It's when the church disappoints you that you start to realize how much you are committed to Jesus and not just a Christian social club. Job wouldn't allow the setbacks he faced to sabotage the relationship he treasured with God.

We must also refuse to allow disappointments to cancel out future appointments. So how do we handle the disappointment? How do we keep following when we feel like quitting? Take a moment to read these beautiful words with me:

> Though the cherry trees don't blossom
>   and the strawberries don't ripen,
> Though the apples are worm-eaten
>   and the wheat fields stunted,
> Though the sheep pens are sheepless
>   and the cattle barns empty,
> I'm singing joyful praise to God.
>   I'm turning cartwheels of joy to my Savior God.
> Counting on God's Rule to prevail,
>   I take heart and gain strength.
> I run like a deer.
>   I feel like I'm king of the mountain! (Habakkuk 3:17-19 MSG).

We can return to these verses again and again as medicine to our soul in times of disappointment. The prophet is telling us to choose our focus. God's faithfulness isn't affected by our temporary changing circumstances. The betrayal of a friend does not alter the unchanging love of God. In disappointment, the choice to praise and give thanks puts the emphasis not on what is lost but on what God has already given. Like Job, and like Habakkuk, even in seasons of affliction we can count on "God's Rule to prevail." Even disappointment can bear eternal fruit if you choose to keep following after Him.

Look again at Habakkuk 3:17-19. Write your own song of praise to God, describing your experience of worship in your own circumstances.

DARE TO FOLLOW IN OPPORTUNITY

—— Natalie ——

We are God's masterpiece. He has created us anew in Christ Jesus,
so we can do the good things he planned for us long ago.

EPHESIANS 2:10 NLT

Is your progress hindered by the possibility of failure, or the chance that you might succeed? What do you do when God gives you the opportunity you've been waiting for? We can become so accustomed to the struggles of the valley that we resist experiencing the "mountaintop moments," as if they're too good to be true. Other times, we respond by taking the opportunity and running with it, leaving Jesus behind entirely. Following Jesus isn't just for the difficult seasons, when it's obvious that we need His help. It's for the moments of opportunity as well. If we're not keeping our eyes fixed on Jesus, we end up striving to hold on to what we have rather than enjoying it.

His divine power has given us everything we need for a godly life through our knowledge of him who called us by his own glory and goodness (2 Peter 1:3).

Scripture promises that God's divine power will give us what we need to live a godly life. We cannot achieve it in our own strength. This is easy to understand as we walk through difficult seasons and lean into His power and strength, but it's also important to remember as we walk into seasons of opportunity. When we step into what God has brought us to, it will always be a larger space than we can fill. He does this on purpose so that we continue to remain in Him and rely on Him.

Don't mistake the moments of opportunity for God's goodness. He is good in every season. When we trust in Him and not in our circumstances, we get to experience all that He has. We don't have to be afraid of new opportunities and we don't have to strive for them, but we can operate from a place of peace and rest. It's as true on the mountaintop as it is in the valley: The only way to keep moving forward is to keep your eyes fixed on Jesus.

How have you been tempted

to rely on your own strength

and abilities in seasons of

plenty and opportunity?

How did God show you your

need for Him even in those

mountaintop moments?

DARE TO FOLLOW IN THE KNOWN

—— *Charlotte* ——

Then the LORD called Samuel. Samuel answered, "Here I am." And he ran to Eli and said, "Here I am; you called me." But Eli said, "I did not call; go back and lie down."

1 SAMUEL 3:4-5

When things become familiar, we can forget to follow. We start to allow routine to become the leader and soon establish patterns that become well-worn ruts. We tread them daily, so familiar with our usual that we don't expect God to say anything new.

Eli had served God all his life, and on the night described in today's verses, he was lying down in his usual place. When a voice started calling his young student, Samuel, Eli did not discern that God was speaking. His usual place was keeping him from this unusual interruption.

Could it be that we often also lay down in the usual place—the place of the known, the expected, the managed? We may be serving God, even leading people in the things of God, and yet our mindset can be so familiar that we miss the voice calling us to follow. Eli knew God's voice, but this was the time he simply expected to get some rest. We can start to schedule God into our routine, have places where we make the time to meet with Him, but what if God wants to wake us in the night? What if He wants to speak to us when a conversation isn't on our schedule? We have to make sure the predictability of our schedules doesn't shrink the capacity of the God-centered life we are called to live.

Have you ever been surprised when someone you thought you knew did something completely out of character? We can develop a blind spot, predicting outcomes based on our incomplete knowledge of a person. We must make sure that in familiar places we remain flexible. We serve a God who is constantly calling us deeper and higher, which means we should be open to being enlarged and stretched—doing something out of character for ourselves!

If you feel life is mundane and boring, maybe you have become stuck in the ruts you've created. You have replaced the adventure of following God with a schedule of visiting God. God has more to reveal to you, so today, where do you need to allow God to get you out of the usual place into a wide-open space? In a life that is known, don't lose sight of the God who knows the path He has laid out for you.

Where can you change your mindset from one of familiar to one of wonder, from one of scheduling to one of seeking?

DAY 97

DARE TO FOLLOW IN THE UNKNOWN

———— Natalie ————

When he has brought out all his own, he goes on ahead of them,
and his sheep follow him because they know his voice.

JOHN 10:4

Scripture tells us the Word is a lamp unto our feet, but sometimes we still feel like we're stumbling around in the dark. It can seem like we're wandering aimlessly, just trying to find the target, let alone a bullseye. Maybe you're in a season where this feels true right now and you've picked up this book in an attempt to find some direction. Be encouraged! You might not know where you're headed, but when you're following Jesus, you can trust that you are always moving in the right direction.

In John 10, Jesus talks about Himself as our good Shepherd. We are His sheep, and He is our provider, protector, and the one who leads the way. This passage doesn't just speak to who He is to us; it also speaks to who we are as His sheep. We know His voice and we follow Him, not the voice of a stranger. When you aren't sure where to go, if you're moving in the right direction, or if you even know what God is saying, take heart. His Word is true. Our hearing and discernment must be sharpened, and it certainly takes practice, but the truth of the Word of God goes beyond what we are able to understand. Even though we might think we are wandering, we are not lost. And even if we have strayed, He always leaves the 99 sheep to find the one. No matter how lost we feel, we are never far from God's sight.

Following Jesus isn't always easy and we're not always sure that we're doing it right, but we can always be sure of Him and what He says in His Word. We may doubt ourselves and His promises, but we can be confident that He who began a good work in us will bring it to completion. We just have to keep showing up with what we have, following Him, and He will lead us in the way everlasting.

In your daily walk with God, how do you recognize the Shepherd's voice?

DARE TO FOLLOW IN SUCCESS

—— *Charlotte* ——

I have learned to be content whatever the circumstances. I know what it is to be in need, and I know what it is to have plenty. I have learned the secret of being content in any and every situation, whether well fed or hungry, whether living in plenty or in want.

PHILIPPIANS 4:11-12

What is success? Who gets to define whether you win or lose in life? So often success is a moving target that we allow social media, popular opinion, company pressure, or educational institutions to measure. Yet when we read the Word of God, we find no such measuring chart. Following Christ is not about success; it's all about surrender.

Success is often a great revealer of a person's heart. It's in the moments of victory that we see who wants the glory. When Saul was successful and chosen by the people as king, he built monuments in his image. When David was successful, he offered burnt sacrifices to thank God for the victory. If success matters more than surrender, we will constantly seek to please people rather than God.

In a life spent collecting accolades, a commitment to following Christ will be difficult to sustain. A surrendered life will often look like the opposite of worldly success, but it is one of true fulfillment.

The apostle Paul discovered that fulfillment, and he described it as contentment. Contentment might not sound as attractive as success, and yet living a contented life means no matter the circumstances, you win. You are immune from the highs and lows of a life spent striving after success. You are content if people applaud you, and you are content if people ignore you.

Jesus died betrayed and hanging on a criminal's cross, yet we know this was the greatest victory ever won. Success doesn't desire a crown of thorns, and it doesn't seek after the thorn in the flesh that Paul describes in 2 Corinthians 12. Yet these thorns we encounter as we follow Christ become the very places where we experience the real victories.

Today, examine the things you are chasing. If they are temporary trinkets, then it's time to change your focus; don't allow what is temporary to demand so much energy. If we can journey the pathway of contentment, we may find the secret of real fulfilment—the discovery that all we need is in Him and that everything we have belongs to Him.

Write out a prayer renewing your commitment to follow after Jesus, no matter the cost.

Charlotte Gambill has an infectious love for life, a deep love for people, and zealous love for God's House. Her passion is to build the local church across the earth, to see people reach their full potential, and to develop and strengthen leadership. Charlotte is known for her practical, humorous, and passionate application of God's Word. Her messages of life and purpose are rallying a generation to embrace the broken and become ambassadors of hope. Charlotte is an author, speaker, pastor, and mother. She leads LIFE Church, UK, in England with her husband, Steve, and together they have two children, Hope Cherish and Noah Brave.

As an eight-time GRAMMY® nominee and five-time GMA Dove Awards Female Vocalist of the Year, **Natalie Grant** has become an icon in Christian and Gospel music. In addition to garnering more than 500 million streams and multiple #1 albums and singles on the Billboard Charts, she is also a respected author and philanthropist. She is the cofounder of Hope for Justice, a nonprofit organization in the fight against human trafficking, which has 32 offices across 9 countries and 5 continents and has helped 102,803 children in the last year.

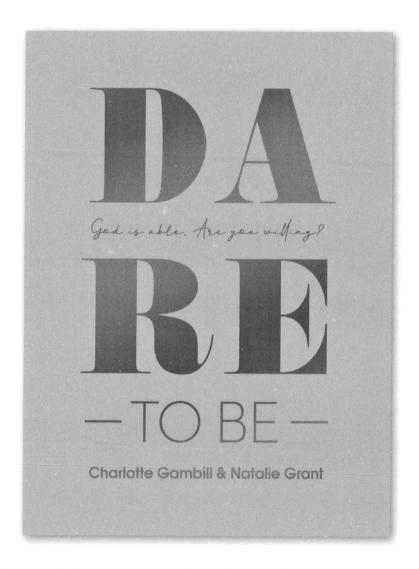

DARE

God is able. Are you willing?

RE

— TO BE —

Charlotte Gambill & Natalie Grant

When was the last time you stepped out of your comfort zone? Have you ever realized God wasn't saying *no* or *wait*, but was instead asking you to act out in courage? *Dare to Be* will challenge you to break away from the mundane and start living to magnify the One who wants you to fulfill your divine destiny.